Edexcel GCSE

Business Studies

Neil Denby

My grateful thanks to Dr R. S. (Bob) Johnson for his technical expertise and advice
Neil Denby

Philip Allan Updates, an imprint of Hodder Education, an Hachette UK company, Market Place, Deddington, Oxfordshire OX15 0SE

Orders
Bookpoint Ltd, 130 Milton Park, Abingdon, Oxfordshire OX14 4SB
tel: 01235 827720
fax: 01235 400454
e-mail: uk.orders@bookpoint.co.uk
Lines are open 9.00 a.m.–5.00 p.m., Monday to Saturday, with a 24-hour message answering service. You can also order through the Philip Allan Updates website: www.philipallan.co.uk

Copyright © 2010 Neil Denby
ISBN 978-1-4441-0777-7

First printed 2010
Impression number   5   4   3   2   1
Year   2014   2013   2012   2011   2010

Printed in Italy

Hachette UK's policy is to use papers that are natural, renewable and recyclable products and made from wood grown in sustainable forests. The logging and manufacturing processes are expected to conform to the environmental regulations of the country of origin.

P01686

Contents

Introduction

How to revise

Revision is not just about remembering, but about being able to apply what you have remembered to business situations. You should, therefore, make sure that you do not just learn facts, but know how a business would use them in its decision making. There are very few questions that will ask you for straightforward knowledge.

10 tips for effective revision

1 Start revising in plenty of time. You may have to revisit some topics at the last minute, but you should try to make sure there are only a few of these.
2 Have a set time and place, where you cannot be disturbed, for your revision sessions.
3 Plan revision carefully — make sure you leave enough time to cover everything.
4 Plan short-term targets — 'I will have learnt *xxx* by *xxx*.' These show you are making progress and help to motivate you.
5 Do not do too much! Your brain needs regular rests in order to be able to process and store information properly.
6 Revise topics three times. This will help to put the knowledge into your long-term memory.
7 Make sure your revision is active — make notes, use spider diagrams, pictograms and mind maps, write raps or lyrics. Sound and visual reminders are usually better than just words.
8 Think about using new technology. You could make a podcast of a revision topic and listen to it on your MP3 player.
9 Practise applying your knowledge to business situations. Use the questions in this book to practise your examination technique. Make sure you draw on all the relevant information, not just a single topic.
10 Revise with someone else — then you can test each other, compare notes, etc.

How to use this book

Each chapter in the book is short and contains the basic knowledge you will need to pass at GCSE. In each chapter there are a number of features.

■ *What the specification requires.* This tells you the sort of knowledge that the specification needs you to know, and steers you in the direction of the types of question that can be asked.

- *In brief.* This states the knowledge requirement in a couple of sentences. For last-minute refreshers, this is what you will need.

- *Revision notes.* This feature outlines the area of knowledge that it is absolutely essential for you to know about each topic.

- *Speak the language.* This gives the key terms and definitions that you will need for a particular topic. In all GCSE business examinations, there are marks for using the correct technical language. These are highlighted in the text.

- *In a nutshell.* This contains the key points from the topic as a bullet list.

- *Boost your grade.* This feature tells you how to access AO1 knowledge marks or how to move from AO1 to AO2 explanation and context marks or from AO2 to AO3 analysis, recommendation and judgement marks.

- *Test yourself.* This provides a short test on the content of all or part of the topic. It takes the form of multiple-choice questions, missing-word questions or tests that you can self-set.

At the end of each section, you will find a longer question, a set of multiple-choice questions or a similar exercise to test your knowledge. At the end of each unit, you will find a full practice examination paper, just like the one that you will sit for your GCSE.

Suggested answers to all the questions are available online at:
www.hodderplus.co.uk/philipallan.

Edexcel GCSE Business Studies

The Edexcel GCSE Business Studies qualification is not one GCSE, but several. There is a 'suite' of units to choose from and different ways to achieve the qualification. The choices that you make can lead you to a short-course qualification (half a GCSE) or a full-course single GCSE qualification in Business Studies; Business Studies and Economics; or Business and Communications. This guide covers the examined units of the Business Studies qualification. There is also an Applied Business qualification, which is not covered in this book (although the Finance chapters in this guide cover all of the examined units of the Applied GCSE).

The routes to a qualification are:
Unit 1 + Unit 2 + Unit 3 = GCSE Business Studies
Unit 1 + Unit 2 + Unit 5 = GCSE Business Studies and Economics
Unit 1 + Unit 2 + Unit 4 = GCSE Business Communications
Unit 1 (examined as Unit 6) + Unit 2 = GCSE Business Studies Short Course

In each case the core unit, and the first one likely to be taught, is Unit 1.

Unit 1 Introduction to small business

Unit 1 is a compulsory unit for all routes. It is examined with a single paper, consisting mostly of multiple-choice questions to test your knowledge. The unit contains five sections. These are:
- Spotting a business opportunity
- Showing enterprise

- Putting a business idea into practice
- Making the start-up effective
- Understanding the economic context

Spotting a business opportunity

This topic covers how an entrepreneur goes about finding a new business opportunity by gaining an insight into a potential business's customers, its market and its competitors. The topic looks at customer needs and how a business could find out about such needs through market research. It goes on to study the buying habits of customers and to look at how customers make up a market. Having identified a gap in the market, the entrepreneur then needs to analyse competitors' strengths and weaknesses so that the business can compete effectively against them. Entrepreneurs must then understand both why to add value and how it can be added. Finally, this topic looks at how a business could reduce its risk of failure, by taking the franchise route.

Showing enterprise

This topic covers the skills that a budding entrepreneur might need, particularly the ability to think creatively and solve problems. It covers definitions of enterprise and entrepreneurs, and the creative and innovative skills that successful entrepreneurs possess. In particular, it covers the nature of risk and risk taking, particularly how entrepreneurs take calculated risks in the hope of gaining rewards. Finally, you can try to apply the skills that you have learned to a business start-up of your own.

Putting a business idea into practice

This topic covers how to make a business idea into a reality, particularly the financial steps that may need to be taken. It looks at objectives, both financial and non-financial, and then at the finances of the business. How, for example, does an owner estimate cost, revenue and profit, and use tools such as cash-flow forecasts?

Making the start-up effective

This topic covers the other people who are essential to the success of a business — its staff and its customers. The topic looks at how to understand the customer base and how to balance the marketing mix in order both to attract and to retain customers. Customer service and customer satisfaction are also investigated. Further topics include the recruitment, training and motivation of staff for a business. The topic also looks at the legal and tax issues attached to working as a sole trader or another form of business organisation.

Understanding the economic context

This topic covers the external economic factors that underpin all business activity. Factors such as changes in interest rates, exchange rates, international currency rates and commodity prices are investigated in terms of their impact on small businesses (changes in exchange rates are limited to the US dollar and the European Union euro). This area also covers the effect of business cycles on the business and the influence of its stakeholders.

Unit 2 Investigating small business

This unit has the same content as Unit 1 but is assessed through a controlled assessment. Pages 137–38 of this book contain advice on how to tackle this unit.

Unit 3 Building a business

This unit investigates how a business might develop once it has been established. It looks at larger businesses, growth and international issues that face businesses. It consists of five sections:

- Marketing
- Meeting customer needs
- Effective financial management
- Effective people management
- External influences on business

Marketing

This topic looks at how a business can compete effectively against the other businesses in its market. What do businesses mean by 'competitive advantage' and how can they gain it over their rivals? The topic covers the collection and interpretation of market research data, and how these can be fed into the marketing mix. It looks at how to persuade customers to try a product for the first time, and how to provide a sufficiently good experience — and enough value — for them to become repeat customers. The topic also looks at the product life cycle and the importance of branding.

Meeting customer needs

This topic covers how the product can meet customer needs and result in a satisfied customer. Customer service is a major element of this, but it also includes effective stock management, so that customers are not disappointed, and effective quality control and standards. It is important to follow the legal requirements of consumer protection law as part of customer service. The tension between the function of a product, its looks and its price is also explored.

Effective financial management

This topic considers how a business can ensure that it is financially sound. It emphasises the decisions that have to be taken by business owners, and the sort of information on which they can make those decisions. In particular, it looks at the analysis and control of cash flow and at the use of breakeven charts to carry out 'what if?' analyses, to predict possible financial changes to the business. It also investigates how a business could improve its profitability and finance its growth.

Effective people management

As the business grows, its organisation will become more complex and the number of people it employs will grow. This topic looks at organisation structures and the effect of good and bad communication within them. It also looks at the different ways in which staff can be paid. Motivation of staff is another important factor in encouraging them to be more efficient at their job.

External influences on business

All businesses are subject to a range of external influences, over which they have no control. They face ethical and environmental questions in the modern world and are expected to operate in a way that is fair and moral, and causes no damage to the environment. This topic looks at the meaning of ethics, how businesses can be environmentally friendly, and how such social responsibility can also make good business sense. It also investigates some of the issues of international trade, particularly the tensions between the developed and the developing world. Government and EU regulation of business is the area considered.

Further study

The specification is designed to get you to think about how, practically, you could become involved in business as an entrepreneur or stakeholder. It also acts as a springboard for further study for AS or A-level.

Unit 1
Introduction to small business

Topic 1

Understanding customer needs and the market

What the specification requires

You need to recognise that a successful business understands both its customers and the market in which it is operating. It can use market research to find out about both. It can also use business techniques such as market mapping to spot a **gap in a market**.

In brief

A market is anywhere that a buyer and seller come together to agree on a sale. The business that is doing the selling needs to know as much as possible about the customer who is doing the buying in order to succeed. Most businesses succeed by either finding or creating a gap in the market — by offering a product that is wanted, but which other businesses do not provide. They are likely to target particular parts of a market, called market segments.

Revision notes

- Making sure that the business knows what customers want, and then providing it, is essential to success. By providing products to the customers who want them, businesses are operating in a market.
- A market is anywhere that buyers and sellers come together to agree on the price for an amount of a product. This does not have to be a physical place: markets can take place via telephone or online. A product will be either a **good** or a **service**. Goods are things that can be touched; services are done for or to a customer.
- New businesses look for a gap in the market. A gap in the market is where a **demand** exists, but it is not being met. Businesses can map their market by listing its key features, then seeing where there are gaps.
- Some businesses are able to create a gap in the market by, for example, offering a completely new type of product.
- Market research may be collected from published sources (secondary) or may be original (primary), such as interviews and questionnaires. One important source of such data is direct customer contact and feedback.

Just one sort of market — wit products, demand and supply

- Markets are often divided into segments. These can then be more easily targeted. Common ways to segment markets are by age, geography, gender, hobbies and interests, and socioeconomic groups (i.e. the level of income and education enjoyed by a household).
- Market research may produce both quantitative and qualitative data. Quantitative data involve numbers and statistics. Qualitative data involve opinions, views and interpretations.

Speak the language

gap in the market — where there is demand, but no product to fill it

goods — those things that can be 'touched'

services — those things done to or for a customer

demand — the amount of products and services customers are willing to pay for

In a nutshell

* Businesses provide products to markets.
* To succeed, they need to find a gap in the market.
* This means analysing the market — both buyers and sellers.
* This can be achieved through market research.
* Generally businesses are set up to make a profit.
* Profit is the surplus of revenue over costs and the reward for the entrepreneur.

Boost your grade

AO1: to access Level 1 marks you need to understand that the most important part of a business transaction is usually the customer. Being able to explain that keeping the customer happy is the basis for business success will give you AO1 marks.

Test yourself

Fill in the missing words from the list below. If you are feeling confident, cover the words and do the exercise from memory.

Businesses are set up in order to provide the .... that people need and want.

Businesses sell and customers buy. This is called a .... Goods are things that can be 'touched' as opposed to things done for or to a customer, called ....

Markets are often divided into .... These can then be more easily targeted.

Common ways of .... include age, geography, gender, hobbies and interests, and .... (i.e. the level of income and education enjoyed by a household).

Market research may produce both ...., involving numbers and statistics, and ...., involving opinions, views and interpretations.

> market   products   qualitative data   quantitative data
> segmentation   segments   services   socioeconomic groups

Topic 2
Understanding added value

What the specification requires

You need to recognise that a successful business understands its competitors and knows about their strengths and weaknesses. This allows it to compete effectively by offering a **unique selling point** or by providing better value for money than its rivals. Successful businesses know how to add value.

In brief

Businesses have to compete for customers with other businesses. Customers usually have a choice and will buy from the business that offers them the best value for money. Products will be designed to have unique selling points, to appeal to the target market by offering greater value than those of rivals. Businesses can add value in a number of ways. They can provide convenience, such as different ways to make payment, or car parking or delivery services. They can offer to provide products or carry out services faster and more efficiently than rivals. They can also provide specific design features.

Revision notes

- Most businesses will face some form of competition. Sometimes this is obvious, such as two butcher shops in a village. These are in direct competition.
- Sometimes competition is less obvious. There may be just one butcher in the village, but this is competing with butchers in other villages, supermarkets and even the internet. It is also competing with all those products that could be eaten instead of meat.
- Customers always have a choice — they can always choose to go without the product that you are selling.
- New businesses need to analyse the strengths and weaknesses of competitors.
- They can build **competitor profiles** by identifying both local and national (and even international) competitors.
- Competitors can be found by using business directories, telephone listings and search engines on the internet.

Butchers may be in competition with the local supermarket

- The strengths and weaknesses of businesses can be found by reading company reports, by reading reports written on them by other competitors and by observation.
- One effective way to judge competitors is to be one of their customers. You can then see what choice they are offering, what their unique selling point is, and how they treat their customers. Such research and observations can also reveal further opportunities by showing gaps in markets.
- Businesses can compete by **adding value** to a product. This means making sure customers receive, or think that they receive, better value for money than from a competitor. Common ways to add value are good service, convenience, different ways to pay, speed and efficiency, and design features. Brands are also used to indicate added value.

In a nutshell

* Businesses are all in competition.
* Customers can choose which business to buy from.
* New businesses need to analyse their possible competitors.
* They can do this through research and observation.
* Businesses can add value to a product in a number of ways.
* Added value will attract customers to a business instead of to its competitor.

Speak the language

unique selling point — the factor that only your business or product has, which makes it stand out

competitor profile — research to show where competitors are found and how they are competing

adding value — making a product worth more to a customer

Test yourself

Almost all of the questions in your Unit 1 examination will be multiple-choice questions. Choose the most appropriate answer from each of the choices below.

1 New businesses need to analyse the strengths and weaknesses of competitors because: **(a)** they need to employ people, **(b)** they will be able to compete more effectively, **(c)** they are on the high street, **(d)** they have internet access.

2 Adding value to a product means that a customer receives which of the following? **(a)** competitor value, **(b)** more value for money, **(c)** more products, **(d)** better service

3 The factor that makes your business stand out is called **(a)** the unique sticking point, **(b)** the unique sticking place, **(c)** the unique selling point, **(d)** the unique selling place.

4 Businesses can add value through all of the following *except*: **(a)** increasing price, **(b)** better service, **(c)** increasing product range, **(d)** providing ways to pay.

5 Brands may be used to indicate which of the following to customers? **(a)** better service, **(b)** better products, **(c)** added competition, **(d)** added value

AO1: you can often access basic AO1 marks just by using the knowledge you have from your own experience. Think about who is competing against whom in your local town, or shopping centre. Then think about which shops you use, and how they have added enough value to persuade you to buy from them.

Topic 3
Franchising

What the specification requires

You need to know and understand why a person starting up a business might operate as a franchisee. You need to understand that there are both advantages and disadvantages to being part of a franchise, rather than setting up an independent business. You should understand that there are other start-up options.

In brief

Franchising is when a successful business decides to expand by selling the right to other businesses to set up using its ideas. A **franchise** is a way of starting, owning and operating a business without the high levels of risk that may be associated with other types of start-up. A franchise is a way to organise a business rather than a form of business ownership. It helps the person selling the franchise to expand and gives the person buying the franchise a much better chance of surviving and succeeding.

Revision notes

- A franchise is permission to sell a product (good or service) or brand, or to use the successful format of an existing business.
- There are two key players in a franchise. The **franchisee** buys into the success of the established business, buying the use of its name, its brand, its advertising, its reputation and its support. The **franchiser** is the seller of the franchise that has a successful product, brand or format.

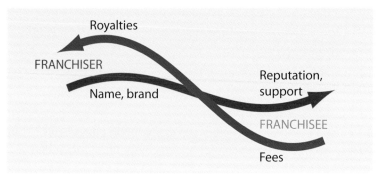

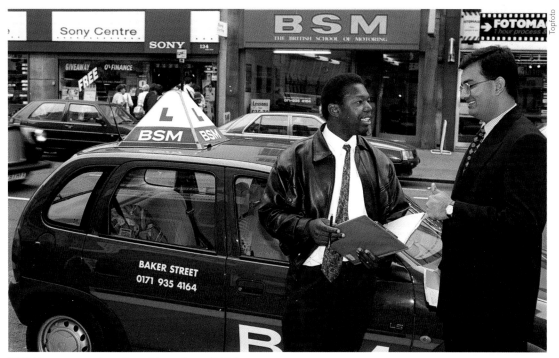

BSM instructors buy franchises from BSM

- Franchisers charge a fee for the franchise and collect a **royalty**, usually based on a percentage of the annual sales of the franchisee. Because a franchisee is buying into a successful product, the fee for the franchise can often be quite high and competition to buy a franchise quite fierce.
- Franchisers may be quite restrictive — insisting on particular suppliers, and making sure that uniforms, products and services are identical.
- The advantage to franchisees is that they buy into an established business and may receive help with products, staff, training, marketing and sales materials. They are much more likely to succeed. Franchisees may also gain an exclusive territory, away from competition for the same brand. The disadvantage is that there may be restrictions on how the business is run.
- The advantage to the franchiser is that their idea or brand is spread. Franchising is a way to expand the business. Franchisers also receive an income from the franchisee. One disadvantage is that a poor franchisee may harm their reputation.
- Starting as a franchise might remove some of the independence of a business, so some businesses will prefer to start as sole traders (single, independent owners) or partnerships (two or more independent owners).

> **Speak the language**
>
> **franchise** — permission to use a successful business format
>
> **franchisee** — the buyer of the franchise
>
> **franchiser** — the seller of the franchise
>
> **royalty** — a percentage of the franchisee's income taken as payment by the franchiser

In a nutshell

* A franchise is a form of business organisation.
* Franchisees buy the right to use the franchiser's name and reputation.
* Franchisers gain by expanding their business and receiving fees.
* Franchisers gain by being much more likely to succeed.
* Businesses may find franchising restrictive, and choose to stay independent.

Test yourself

Choose the most appropriate answer from each of the choices below.

1 A franchisee is **(a)** the seller of the franchise, **(b)** the buyer of the franchise, **(c)** the owner of the brand, **(d)** a customer of the franchise.

2 A royalty is **(a)** a set amount, **(b)** based on a percentage, **(c)** Burger King, **(d)** fixed each year.

3 If a franchisee harms the reputation of the franchise, this is **(a)** an advantage to the franchiser, **(b)** an advantage to the franchisee, **(c)** a disadvantage to the franchiser, **(d)** a disadvantage to the franchisee.

4 Franchises can help new businesses to **(a)** set up, **(b)** borrow money, **(c)** reduce risk, **(d)** expand.

5 Franchises can help successful businesses to **(a)** set up, **(b)** borrow money, **(c)** reduce risk, **(d)** expand.

Topic 4
Locating a start-up

What the specification requires

Businesses need to take a number of key decisions when setting up. You will need to learn about and understand the factors that influence the choice of a start-up business location. These include **start-up costs**, how easy it is to access both raw materials and the intended market, whether or not transport, labour and the right technology are all available, and likely levels of competition.

In brief

Businesses need to decide not only what they are going to sell, but also from where they are going to sell it. One of the most important decisions that an **entrepreneur** has to make is where the business will be based. Several factors may influence this. For some businesses, a single factor will stand out; for others, a combination of factors will be important. For many, the nature of the good or service they are selling is key. All businesses, even the smallest online ones, need to have somewhere from which to trade.

Revision notes

- There are many factors that influence location.
- The ideal location will not be too expensive, but will help the business to attract customers.
- There are government grants and other assistance packages to help businesses set up in certain areas. The EU also provides regional assistance.
- Franchise start-ups may be restricted by the franchiser to particular areas or territories. This could be seen as an advantage — cutting down competition — but could also restrict growth. Franchisers do not want franchisees competing with each other.

Dell only sells online

- Customers may need to visit a shop or other **retail outlet**. Such outlets need display and storage space along with parking or public transport for customers.
- Internet shopping lets customers view stock and buy online, so some businesses have done away with other retail outlets.
- Service providers (such as plumbers and hairdressers) must be close to their markets.
- Good transport or **infrastructure** links are vital for both suppliers and customers. Suppliers need access to bring materials in; customers need to be able to reach the business.
- In some cases, a business may need a large workforce, or may need a workforce with particular qualifications, skills or specialisms.
- Having competitors close by can bring benefits to a business, as people 'shop around'. It can also make it easier to work with suppliers. However, in other cases, businesses will need to locate away from competitors.

In modern businesses, new technology for communications is vital (such as a broadband connection).

Speak the language

start-up costs — the initial costs paid once when a business is first set up

entrepreneur — the person who takes the risk by starting a business

retail outlet — anywhere that something is sold to a consumer (e.g. shop, vending machine)

infrastructure — roads, railways, airports, power, communications

In a nutshell

All businesses must operate from somewhere, even if it is only the spare bedroom! Where they operate from depends on the nature of the product, process or service they are selling. Location factors for a new business include:

* cost, including national and international government assistance
* raw material availability
* location and ease of access for customers
* location and ease of access for suppliers
* location and skills of workers
* location and strength of competition
* availability of the right technology

Boost your grade   **AO3:** to reach AO3 marks you must show that you can analyse (weigh up both sides of an argument) and judge (come to a decision). There is not always a right or wrong answer, so if you are asked to compare two locations for a business, you should weigh up the good and bad points of each, make a decision, and say why you have made it (justification).

Test yourself

Choose the most appropriate answer from each of the choices below.

1 The costs a business pays once, when it is first established, are called **(a)** start-up costs, **(b)** set-up costs, **(c)** beginning costs, **(d)** establishment costs.

2 A business's location may depend on whether it sells goods or **(a)** clothes, **(b)** food, **(c)** services, **(d)** products.

3 A business extracting raw materials will be located **(a)** on the high street, **(b)** near customers, **(c)** near technology, **(d)** near raw materials.

4 Service providers need to locate close to **(a)** shops, **(b)** markets, **(c)** raw materials, **(d)** technology.

5 National and international help for new businesses can help keep down **(a)** revenue, **(b)** costs, **(c)** customers, **(d)** taxes.

Section test: Spotting a business opportunity

The Edexcel Unit 1 paper is almost all multiple-choice questions. It consists of 20 questions and lasts just 45 minutes. It is meant to test knowledge, rather than skills or application.

1 Which of the following is NOT a major cause of business failure?
  (a) no market for the product
  (b) sales forecasts too optimistic
  (c) not enough debt
  (d) not enough money
  (e) costs higher than anticipated

2 New businesses need to analyse the strengths and weaknesses of competitors because
  (a) they need to employ people
  (b) they will be able to compete more effectively
  (c) they are on the high street
  (d) they have many similar products to sell
  (e) they have internet access

3 The person who sells a franchise is called the
  (a) franchisee
  (b) franchiser
  (c) employer
  (d) employee
  (e) entrepreneur

4 The person who buys a franchise is called the
  (a) franchisee
  (b) franchiser
  (c) employer
  (d) employee
  (e) entrepreneur

5 Which of the following would NOT be an appropriate method of market research for a new small business?
   (a) using published statistics about competitors
   (b) asking customers to fill in a short questionnaire
   (c) employing a specialist company to survey 40,000 people
   (d) asking customers to give brief feedback on service
   (e) interviewing a focus group of customers

6 The initial payment made to buy a franchise is called a
   (a) wage   (d) royalty
   (b) salary   (e) cost
   (c) fee

7 Brands may be used to indicate which of the following to customers?
   (a) better service   (d) added competition
   (b) better products   (e) added value
   (c) better names

8 Why is customer service important to the success of small businesses?
   (a) because the government says so
   (b) because customers add value
   (c) because a small business needs loyalty
   (d) because they sell many products
   (e) because it has to obey the law

9 The ongoing franchise payment that is linked to turnover is called a
   (a) wage   (d) royalty
   (b) salary   (e) cost
   (c) fee

10 Segmentation is likely to be carried out by all of the following EXCEPT:
   (a) age   (d) geography
   (b) height   (e) income
   (c) gender

Topic 5
Enterprise and entrepreneurs

What the specification requires

You need to know that enterprise involves taking a risk in order to gain a reward. The reward for a successful enterprise is the **profit** made by the business. The name given to those who have enterprise skills is **entrepreneurs**. Entrepreneurs will undertake new ventures either to create or fill a gap in the market.

In brief

Entrepreneurs need to take risks in order to bring new or different products to market. They need to have skills of organisation and planning, and are likely to be creative thinkers. They need to be willing to see businesses fail but still be keen to try out new ideas or new products. A product is a good or service offered for sale.

Revision notes

- Businesses are set up in order to provide the products that people need and want, but which they are not able or willing to provide for themselves.
- By providing products to the customers who want them, businesses are operating in a market.
- A market is anywhere that buyers and sellers come together to agree on the price for an amount of a product. This does not have to be a physical place: markets can take place via telephone or online.
- A product will be either a good or a service. Goods are things that can be touched; services are done for or to a customer.
- Those people who take the risk of starting a business, and provide the organisation, are called entrepreneurs. Their reward, if the business is a success, is profit. Profit is the surplus of income (revenue) over costs.
- Enterprise involves taking risks, but these can be reduced through good planning and research.

Entrepreneur Sir Stelios Haji-Ioannou is the founder of easyJet

- Entrepreneurs look to either find a gap in the market — a product not currently supplied — or create such a gap with an innovative product.
- Not all new enterprises succeed; in fact, many of them fail. An entrepreneur needs to be able to learn from such failures and still be ready to take risks.
- Enterprise skills include teamwork, problem solving, the ability to make connections and see the whole picture, energy and enthusiasm.
- Those businesses providing a community service (such as charities and cooperatives) are called **social enterprises**.

In a nutshell

* Enterprise involves taking a risk in return for a reward.
* There are many enterprise skills, such as teamwork and problem solving.
* Many enterprises fail.
* Risks can be reduced by careful planning.

Boost your grade **AO1:** you will earn AO1 marks for knowledge if you can explain that entrepreneurs can reduce the possibility of failure if they carefully plan their enterprise.

Test yourself

Fill in the missing words from the list below. If you are feeling confident, cover the words and do the exercise from memory.

People who start a business, and provide the ...., are called entrepreneurs. Their ...., if the business is a success, is .... Enterprise involves taking ...., which can be reduced through good .... and research. Not all new enterprises ....; in fact, many of them .... Entrepreneurs need to take .... in order to bring new or different products to market. They need to have skills of organisation and planning, and are likely to be .... Entrepreneurs look either to find a .... — a product not currently supplied — or to create one with an innovative product. Enterprise skills include teamwork, ..., energy and enthusiasm.

creative thinkers   fail   gap in the market   organisation   planning

problem-solving   profit   reward   risks   risks   succeed

Topic 6
Creative thinking and entrepreneurial skill

What the specification requires

You need to understand that business success for start-ups is often linked to being creative. Thinking in a creative way can help both to establish a new business and to ensure that it competes effectively. You should know that entrepreneurs need to use 'what if' scenarios in order to judge between possible alternatives.

In brief

New businesses (especially successful ones) come from new ideas — about products, demand and markets. New ideas can 'just happen' on their own, but they are much more likely to happen as a result of a deliberate decision to think creatively. **Deliberate creativity** is a powerful tool used to assess new business ideas. It can help to encourage innovation in many aspects of development, launch, production and marketing of new products.

Revision notes

- Problem-solving skills are essential to enterprise, and different ways to solve problems need to be devised. One such approach is deliberate creativity.
- Deliberate creativity means making a conscious effort to be creative about a solution. It works on the basis of taking the facts and knowledge that you (or an entrepreneur) have, and the skills that you (or the entrepreneur) have and then applying them to solve a problem.
- One way to look creatively at a problem is by thinking laterally about it. **Lateral thinking** means thinking 'outside the box' — in other words, trying to find solutions to problems and questions by trying new routes. It is about finding different, more creative solutions to problems. Such creative solutions can, in business, lead to new ideas for products, markets, promotions and so on.

Thinking about problems before they happen is a vital enterprise skill

- Such thinking and solutions can help a business to gain a competitive advantage over its rivals.
- Entrepreneurs need to develop creative skills in order to solve problems. They need to think through 'what if' scenarios and judge what might happen in particular situations.
- A 'what if?' scenario is when a person asks a 'what if?' question, such as 'what if demand fell?' or 'what if my main competitor lowered its price?', then works through what might happen so that possible — creative — solutions can be put in place. This is called being **proactive** rather than **reactive**.
- Entrepreneurs also need to ask such questions about new ideas. What would work? Why would it work? What might get in the way?

In a nutshell

* Entrepreneurs have many skills, one of which is problem-solving.
* Problems can often be solved using creative and imaginative approaches.
* These include deliberate creativity and lateral thinking.
* 'What if?' scenarios can be used to anticipate problems and have creative solutions already in place.

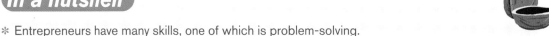

Boost your grade **AO1:** think about how you could be creative in your ideas if you were setting up your own business. This will help you to answer questions about ideas like creativity and lateral thinking.

Test yourself

Match the term on the left with the most suitable phrase on the right.

1	creative solutions	essential enterprise skill
2	deliberate creativity	proactive
3	problem-solving	outside the box
4	lateral thinking	competitive advantage
5	'what if?' scenario	consciously trying to be creative

Topic 7
Invention, innovation and protection

What the specification requires

You need to understand that new business ideas are often the result of careful planning and research rather than sudden inspiration. Many ideas involve an entrepreneur or inventor seeing a problem and then working hard to find a solution. Many well-known businesses and brands have been established through this process.

In brief

Business success is often linked to new products or processes. However, success with such ideas is not guaranteed. Entrepreneurs need to ensure that **innovations** are attractive to the market. It can take a lot of hard work (sometimes over a number of years), with many possible solutions tried, before a particular combination of product and price succeeds in a market. Businesses can use legal means to protect their inventions and innovations both at the development stage and later.

Revision notes

- New business ideas are generated from a number of sources. Most often they are generated by an entrepreneur seeing a way to solve a problem or improve a product.
- Completely new products are called **inventions**. These are not guaranteed to be a success, but need an entrepreneur to bring them to the market at a price that people are willing to pay for them.
- Innovation means bringing a new idea or new product successfully to the market. Sometimes this is an invention, sometimes an improvement. Entrepreneurs are usually innovators.
- Some businesses are 'product-led'. This means that they produce a product and then persuade customers that they need it. There are many technological examples, such as personal music players, mobile phones and USB storage devices.

Creative ideas often lead to exciting innovations

- Other businesses are customer-led. This means that they research what customers might want and then develop a product to fit that need. For example, customers want convenience from supermarket shopping, so the supermarkets provide a web ordering and home delivery service.
- Inventions can be legally protected from competition. A new invention (a product, method or process) can be protected by **patent**. This stops competitors from copying it. Commercial property such as trade marks and brand names is also protected. Copyright is provided automatically to all printed and published material, including both writing and images.
- **Intellectual property** is defined as a person's original work, such as music, art, writing, ideas and inventions. This includes words and designs such as logos and slogans.
- The Intellectual Property Office (IPO) deals with all such applications, requests and issues in the UK.

In a nutshell

* Entrepreneurs seek to develop new ideas.
* Sometimes these are inventions (new products or ways of doing things).
* Entrepreneurs innovate with ideas and/or inventions.
* Inventions can be legally protected.
* All original work — intellectual property — is protected.

Test yourself

Give short answers to the following questions.

1 What is a product-led business?

2 What is a customer-led business?

3 How could a business idea be protected from competition?

4 What is intellectual property?

5 What is copyright?

Topic 8
Calculating and managing risk

What the specification requires

You need to understand that, to be effective, a business needs to plan. It needs to do this to calculate and reduce risk. In particular, planning helps the business when it is setting up and raising finance. You need to know the main risks to a business and why they are important. You should be clear about how planning can be used to reduce the risks of failure.

In brief

A new business needs to outline the aims and objectives it intends to achieve. It should describe the methods, staff and products it intends to use to try to achieve them. It should include planning of financial details and forecasts, based on **market research** into the business's chosen market. Risk in all aspects of the business should be estimated — not just finance, but also the products for sale, **marketing strategy**, and the structure and administration of the business. Risk that is estimated and expected can be managed and reduced. A **business plan** could be used to help raise start-up finance.

Revision notes

- Risk can be reduced through good planning, including writing business plans.
- A good business plan lays down the direction that the business will take and outlines aims and objectives for the first couple of years. It is both a working document for the business and an important management tool that should be updated at regular intervals.
- New businesses often need loans from banks to help them start. A business plan is a useful tool to help gain a loan. It also helps in the calculation of risk, so that it can be reduced.

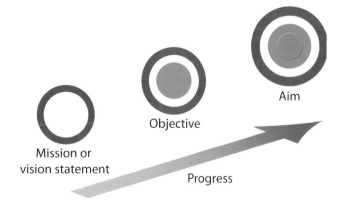

Setting targets helps a business to plan. Targets may be called by different names, depending on how progress is being measured.

- Entrepreneurs often take 'calculated risks'. These are risks where they have estimated possible outcomes. Entrepreneurs will be aware that there are possible downsides to particular actions, but will balance these against possible rewards.
- Calculating risk by weighing up possible outcomes — and the positive and negative sides to them — helps the entrepreneur (and those supporting a start-up, such as a bank) to judge how likely the venture is to succeed.
- New businesses are at risk of failure. Risks include lack of demand for a product, costs that are too high, competition, staff who are not experienced, and not having enough detailed knowledge of the market.
- All of these risks can be reduced but not eliminated. Many businesses fail, and successful entrepreneurs will learn from these failures and not repeat the same mistakes.

In a nutshell

* New businesses often face many risks.
* A business plan and other planning tools help to reduce these risks.
* Risk that is estimated and expected can be managed and reduced.
* Not all new businesses succeed: entrepreneurs will learn from their mistakes.

Boost your grade

AO1 to AO2: you should know about the two elements to risk: first, how likely an event is to occur; and second how bad the consequences would be if it did. The consequences of being in an air crash are severe, but the likelihood is low, so people take the risk. The likelihood of falling off while learning to ride a bike is high, but the consequences of falling off are not severe, so again people take the risk.

Test yourself

Fill in the missing words from the list below. If you are feeling confident, cover the words and do the exercise from memory.

Many .... businesses face the risk of .... A business plan outlines the aims and .... of a business. It helps the business to see where its .... and weaknesses lie. The plan should be based on .... into the business's chosen market. It should include ...., ... and .... details. It is often used to help raise .... by being presented to a .... or other lending institution.

(bank)   (finance)   (financial)   (market)   (market research)
(objectives)   (product)   (start-up)   (failure)   (strengths)

Section test: Showing enterprise

1 Anywhere where buyers and sellers come together to agree a price for a sale is called which of the following?
   (a) an enterprise
   (b) an entrepreneur
   (c) a market
   (d) an organisation
   (e) a profit

2 Which of the following is an important skill for an entrepreneur?
   (a) not being worried about risk
   (b) employing at least five workers
   (c) a willingness to work hard
   (d) a willingness to study business studies
   (e) the ability to raise finance

3 How can an entrepreneur reduce the risk of an enterprise failing? Choose TWO of the following.
   (a) starting it quickly
   (b) forward planning
   (c) having lots of money
   (d) good research
   (e) taking big risks

4 Businesses that are set up to provide a community service, such as charities and cooperatives, are usually called which of the following?
   (a) charity enterprises
   (b) helpful enterprises
   (c) high street enterprises
   (d) social enterprises
   (e) community enterprises

5 Which THREE of the following are the most likely reasons why a person might want to start a business?
   (a) to make a profit
   (b) to work as little as possible
   (c) to achieve an ambition
   (d) to make sure they have an easy life
   (e) to be independent

6 Which TWO of the following are recognised as new ways to solve business problems?
   (a) long-term borrowing
   (b) a change of government
   (c) deliberately lower levels of taxation
   (d) lateral thinking
   (e) deliberate creativity

7 A 'what if?' scenario is when a person asks a 'what if?' question, such as 'what if demand fell?' or 'what if my main competitor lowered its price?', then works through what might happen so that creative solutions can be put in place. This is called being which of the following?
   (a) reactive
   (b) proactive
   (c) inactive
   (d) unactive
   (e) hyperactive

8 Duncan Bannatyne is now a millionaire. He started his first business by buying an ice cream van. Which of the following skills would have most contributed to his success?
   (a) the ability to make ice cream
   (b) demonstrating initiative
   (c) having a lot of money
   (d) being able to drive
   (e) employing several helpers

9 Original work, such as music, art, writing, ideas and inventions, is protected by law because it is all which of the following?
   (a) private property
   (b) community property
   (c) expensive property
   (d) intellectual property
   (e) anybody's property

10 New businesses are often at risk of failure. Which TWO of the following would be considered a risk by a new business set-up?
   (a) lack of demand
   (b) lack of competition
   (c) thorough market research
   (d) staff who are not experienced
   (e) detailed knowledge of the market

Topic 9
What business could I start?

What the specification requires

You should understand that, if you were going to start a business, you would need to plan carefully, calculate possible risks (and possible rewards) and decide on whether the risk was worth taking. You would need to demonstrate **entrepreneurial skills** and qualities if you were going to succeed.

In brief

Using all the information that you have learned about risk, entrepreneurs and entrepreneurial skills, as well as the details about creative thinking and innovation, how would you go about starting your own small business? What qualities do you think that you would need? How could you plan efficiently and do you think that your business idea would be a success? What help would you be able to get to support you in your enterprise?

Revision notes

- Starting a business of your own requires both **creativity** and entrepreneurial skills.
- You would start by trying to identify a **gap in the market** (or you could try to create a gap in the market with a new and innovative product or idea). By researching products that you have bought, you could find out if there is a gap. For example, if you bought a good or service that did not live up to your expectations, is there a way that you could improve it, and sell it yourself?
- Once you have identified a gap in the market, you would need to plan your start-up carefully. You need to think ahead to anticipate problems that might arise, and be ready with possible solutions if they do.

Researching products can help you to identify a gap in the market

- To succeed, you will need to demonstrate determination, energy and commitment. You will need to be prepared to work hard, for long hours. It may be some time before a successful business is profitable, so you will need to forecast income and expenditure, and make sure that you have enough money for your own needs.
- Support is available from organisations such as the government through the Business Start-Up Scheme and through charities like the Prince's Youth Business Trust (usually called the Prince's Trust).
- The government encourages banks to lend, and guarantees some small business loans.

Speak the language

entrepreneurial skills — creativity, willingness to work hard, problem-solving and organisational skills

creativity — the ability to think up new, exciting and innovative solutions to problems

gap in the market — where there is demand for a product but no product yet exists to fulfil that demand

In a nutshell

* Entrepreneurs often learn by trying.
* You could try to start your own business to see if it would succeed.
* You will need to have all the entrepreneurial skills that you have learned.
* Your business may fail, but that should just be used as a learning journey to help you succeed next time.

Test yourself

Give short answers to the following questions.

1 List the skills that you think are essential to entrepreneurial success.

2 Put these in order of priority, with the most important one first, and explain why you think that this is most important.

3 List three types of support that could be available for a new business.

4 What is meant by a 'gap in the market'?

5 Explain the difference between finding a gap and creating one.

AO1: before starting your own business, you would need to consider all the risks and rewards. You may be asked to choose options from a list in the examination. Make sure that you read all of the options, as sometimes the risks outweigh the rewards.

Topic 10
Objectives at start-up

What the specification requires

You need to understand that there may be a range of different motives behind wanting to start a business and that not all of these are financial. Sometimes an entrepreneur just wants job satisfaction, or to be his or her own boss. There will also be financial objectives linked to this, otherwise the business will not survive.

In brief

Entrepreneurs have many different reasons why they might wish to start a business. These often include job satisfaction, through doing something they enjoy or are good at, and independence — being able to work as their own boss. Some entrepreneurs are happy to remain small; others want to expand and increase profits and market share.

Revision notes

- **Financial objectives** may start with making enough money to survive. This is usually thought of as the **breakeven** point, but it can actually take a business many years to break even. This is not a problem as long as any debt is manageable and as long as sales continue to rise. It is vital for the entrepreneur to pay himself or herself for the effort that is being put in, and this is often missed out of financial estimates.
- Once the business does manage to break even, further objectives might include profit or expansion. Some entrepreneurs are determined to make the business grow and be as profitable as possible. Others are happy for the business to remain small, to earn an income that is sufficient for their needs, but to be able to do a job that they like. This is linked, therefore, to non-financial objectives.
- **Non-financial objectives** may be just as important as financial ones. They include independence (wanting to be your own boss), job satisfaction and personal challenge.

Fotolia

Sometimes staying small and independent is more important than growth

- Some businesses are set up with the intention of helping others, or of providing products or sharing profit in a fair way. These are called charities and cooperatives. They are still run as businesses but with aims that reflect the reasons that they were established, so a charity might have the aim of reducing poverty in a certain group of people.
- Entrepreneurs need to be motivated to meet their objectives. They need to be determined, hard-working, able to lead, problem-solvers and willing to take risks. Some entrepreneurs are lucky in bringing an innovation to market at the right time. Many more succeed through careful planning and research.

In a nutshell

* Entrepreneurs have different reasons for starting businesses.
* Their initial objective may just be to survive, or to remain independent.
* There are both financial and non-financial reasons for setting up.
* Sometimes the non-financial reasons are as strong as, or stronger than, the financial reasons.

Test yourself

Read the passage below and answer the three questions based on it, choosing the most likely answer in each case.

Jim Knight left college last year with a business qualification. He has worked for the past year as an office administrator at Tipall's but is bored with the job and feels that he could do better. He is thinking of setting up his own business. He knows a lot about cars, and enjoys tuning engines. He could buy a site that Shell is vacating and set up his own garage, or work for a friend, Hardip, who runs a garage.

1 Jim's main objective for setting up in business is most likely to be **(a)** profit, **(b)** independence, **(c)** expansion, **(d)** shorter working hours.

2 If Jim sets up a garage his main competitor will be **(a)** Tipall's, **(b)** Shell, **(c)** Hardip, **(d)** none of these.

3 Jim has a business qualification from college. This means that he **(a)** will be better at running a business than Hardip, **(b)** should stay employed at Tipall's, **(c)** knows everything about being an entrepreneur, **(d)** has some knowledge he could apply to his new business.

Topic 11
Estimating revenues, costs and profit

What the specification requires

You need to understand that businesses use a range of financial techniques to try to forecast sales revenues and costs, and from these, possible profits or losses. You need to know the different types of cost and to realise that, in many cases, it is impossible to predict revenues and costs accurately, so that profit forecasts are likely to be rough estimates.

In brief

Businesses produce either a good or a service for sale. If it is a good, then there are raw materials and other inputs to pay for. If it is a service, at the very least the business needs to let people know that it exists. In either case, therefore, there are costs. The money that the business receives for its sales is called **revenue**. Business costs are divided into **fixed costs** (also called indirect costs or overheads) and **variable costs**.

Revision notes

- Businesses forecast sales by estimating how much they will sell at a given price. This gives them an idea of how much sales revenue they will make.
- Price is the amount at which a product is offered for sale. Revenue is measured as the number of units sold × price.
- When total revenue is greater than total cost, the business is making a **profit**. When total revenue is less than total cost, the business is making a loss. The point where the amount of total revenue is equal to the amount of total costs is called the **breakeven** point.
- New businesses face start-up costs that are paid once, when the business begins (e.g. when an internet-based business buys a computer). These are also called 'sunk' costs.
- Costs may be fixed or variable. Total cost is fixed cost plus variable cost. Fixed costs do not vary with output. Examples are rent, interest payments and rates. They are

What's it all worth?

paid whether or not a business is producing. Variable costs vary directly with output. Examples are raw materials, packaging, components, ingredients and power.

■ The business and its owner or owners will be affected by profits and losses. Profits may mean the business can expand. They also signal to other businesses that this is a good market in which to compete. Losses do not signal that a business is failing. It may take some time for it to grow revenue enough to make a profit, but it may then be able to recoup its losses.

In a nutshell

* Businesses produce goods or services for sale at a price.
* Sales at that price produce revenue.
* If revenue is greater than cost, the business is in profit.
* If cost is greater than revenue, the business is making a loss.
* Costs can be listed in many different ways.

Test yourself

Try this exam-style question.

Alberus plc runs a well-known chain of high-street shops, selling a range of goods, including clothes, food and household goods. The business also sells services such as insurance and has its own credit card and bank.

Alberus has a number of different revenue sources. It also has different costs.

1 Describe one fixed and one variable cost. *(2 marks)*

2 Describe three possible major revenue sources. *(3 marks)*

3 Explain which revenue source is most important to the business and why. *(5 marks)*

Boost *your grade*

AO1 to AO2: to access AO2 marks, you must explain answers using examples. This is called putting answers 'in context'. You should make every effort to use a business that you know to illustrate your answers.

Understanding and forecasting cash flow

You need to understand the role and importance of cash to a business. You need to understand that cash flows into and out of a business, and these flows need to be managed. You need to know how a business uses cash-flow statements, to understand what cash-flow problems might arise and to be able to suggest solutions.

In brief

A business has a constant flow of cash in and out. Cash comes in through sales revenue and flows out to pay for costs. As well as money, cash includes bank transfers, cheques, and credit- or debit-card transactions. A business needs enough cash to meet its day-to-day needs. The problem with cash is that the flows of it into and out of a business are never equal, so the business needs to manage these **cash flows**.

Revision notes

- Cash comes into a business from sales and other income; it leaves as a result of costs and expenses. If there is more cash coming in than the business needs, this is called a cash surplus. If there is less cash than it needs, this is called a cash shortage.
- A **cash-flow statement** shows past flows of cash into and out of a business. **Cash-flow forecasts** estimate future flows and help a business to predict when it will need to borrow extra cash. By forecasting cash inflows and outflows, businesses can see where there might be shortfalls or excesses, and plan to even these out.

Cash flows can be shown on either a table or a graph

	Jan	Feb	March	April	May	June
Cash brought forward	1,000	1,000	−1,000	−2,000	−5,000	3,000
+ cash from sales	5,000	1,000	2,000	5,000	12,000	8,000
= total cash available	6,000	2,000	1,000	3,000	7,000	11,000
− cash out	5,000	3,000	3,000	8,000	4,000	4,000
= cash to carry forward	1,000	−1,000	−2,000	−5,000	3,000	7,000

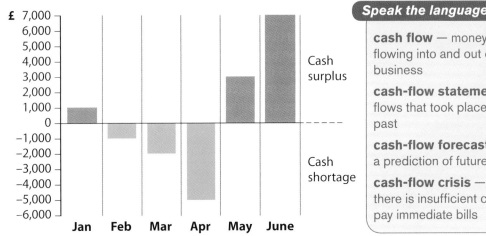

Cash surplus

Cash shortage

Speak the language

cash flow — money flowing into and out of a business

cash-flow statement — flows that took place in the past

cash-flow forecast — a prediction of future flows

cash-flow crisis — when there is insufficient cash to pay immediate bills

- Cash-flow forecasts can help the business see how to avoid problems. Techniques include spreading payments (e.g. making monthly payments rather than facing an annual bill) and arranging to receive revenue more regularly (e.g. getting customers to pay in instalments). Managing cash flow is linked to other issues: for example, cash could be tied up in stock, or be outstanding through sales made on credit. These issues are part of the management of cash flow.
- One of the major reasons for businesses to fail is cash shortages. Even if a business has full order books and is making a profit, it cannot survive if it cannot pay its immediate bills. This is often called a **cash-flow crisis**. This can force a business into failure or insolvency. Having too much cash is also bad for business. Excess cash should be turned into assets that can earn more money.
- Writing a business plan reduces risk, as future problems can be forecast and managed.

In a nutshell

- Cash flows into and out of a business.
- These flows need to be managed.
- Too much cash is a waste of resources.
- Too little cash could lead to business failure.
- Businesses develop techniques to even out cash flows.

AO2 to AO3: with a topic such as cash flow, it is easy to reach AO2 marks by analysing figures. The cash position of a business is changed by a change in revenue or costs. There is therefore a range of possible methods to improve the position by reducing costs or increasing revenue. Remember, though, that most cost reductions have other effects on a business (e.g. cutting staff increases workload for everyone else), and increases in price do not necessarily increase revenue.

Test yourself

Try this exam-style question.

Choose three different businesses, for example:

- a sole trader hairdresser business
- a limited company involved in manufacturing
- a plc supermarket chain

For each, say what are the main inflows and the main outflows of cash. Do not forget loans, whether personal or from banks, and other sources of cash besides sales revenue.

(6 marks)

Topic 13
Obtaining finance

What the specification requires

You should know that small business start-ups do not always find it easy to raise finance. You should be aware of the organisations that support new businesses, and the advice and support that is available. You should learn about the different sources of finance available to a small business, and be able to say when each would be appropriate.

In brief

The money that a business needs may come from its owners, from lenders or people who are willing to take a risk, or from other outside sources. Small businesses will usually start with the owners' own funds as capital. They may also have some inputs from friends and family. Outside of this, it is usual to borrow money. Because small businesses might struggle, there are both government and charitable organisations that might help them.

Revision notes

- Small businesses may have difficulty raising the finance that they need.
- **Owners' funds** are one of the main sources of finance. This is the money that the owners already have. Limited companies can raise funds by selling shares to the owners, who are the shareholders. Owners may also raise finance from friends and family, or from private investors called **venture capitalists**.
- A business may keep some profit for future finance. This is called **retained profit**.
- If business owners do not already have the funds, they will borrow. The most common forms of business borrowing are:
  - trade credit — when a business promises to pay later for goods received now (hopefully, after it has sold them)
  - **overdrafts** — a bank allows the business to take more out of its account than it has deposited, up to an agreed limit; this is flexible and interest is only charged on what is actually owed

> **Speak the language**
>
> **owners' funds** — the money that the owners already have
>
> **venture capitalists** — private investors willing to risk money on new businesses
>
> **retained profit** — profit kept by the business to help finance growth
>
> **overdrafts** — bank permission to withdraw more from an account than has been deposited

- loans — a business borrows a fixed amount, for a fixed term, with regular repayments made and interest charged on the full amount for the term of the loan
- hire-purchase — paying a deposit and buying in instalments (e.g. a vehicle or machine)
- leasing — effectively, renting vehicles, equipment and/or plant
- mortgages — long-term loans used to buy expensive items such as land or buildings, secured on the item bought

■ Business grants may also be available from sources such as the Prince's Trust.

Types of borrowing

Short term (from a few days up to 3 years)	Medium term (from 3 years to 10 years)	Long term (10 years +)
■ Overdrafts	■ Hire-purchase	■ Loans
■ Loans	■ Loans	■ Mortgages
■ Trade credit	■ Debentures	

In a nutshell

* Small businesses are often started with owners' funds.
* Other private sources of finance are also common.
* Otherwise, businesses will borrow from banks.
* The main forms of borrowing are overdrafts and loans.
* Government and charitable bodies provide support to business.

Test yourself

Fill in the missing words from the list below. If you are feeling confident, cover the words and do the exercise from memory.

The money that a business needs often comes from its .... This is called .... Other finance will be raised from lenders such as ....

It may also come from profits kept back or ....

Sometimes people with .... are willing to take a risk on a business. These are called .... Small businesses may also have .... from friends and family. Because small businesses might struggle, there are both .... and charitable organisations that will help them. These include the .... and charities such as ....

(banks) (Business Start-Up Scheme) (capital) (finance) (government) (owners)
(owners' funds) (retained) (the Prince's Trust) (venture capitalists)

Section test: Putting a business idea into practice

1 Which of the following possible sources of finance for a small business would be considered to cost the least?

(a) overdraft

(b) loan

(c) owners' funds

(d) trade credit

(e) mortgage

2 Which of these would be most likely to be the most long-term?

(a) overdraft

(b) loan

(c) owners' funds

(d) trade credit

(e) mortgage

3 Which of these would be most likely to have a term of just 1 or 2 months?

(a) overdraft

(b) loan

(c) owners' funds

(d) trade credit

(e) mortgage

4 Which TWO of the following are examples of fixed costs?

(a) the cost of the power used in the production process

(b) the rent on the premises of the business

(c) buying raw materials for production

(d) the amount spent on advertising a new product

(e) taking out insurance to cover risks to the premises

5 The following table shows a cash-flow forecast for the first 6 months of the year. Fill in the missing figures. *(5 marks)*

	Jan	Feb	March	April	May	June
Cash brought forward	1,000	?	−1,000	−4,000	−9,000	−1,000
+ cash from sales	5,000	1,000	2,000	5,000	12,000	8,000
= total cash available	6,000	2,000	−1,000	?	3,000	7,000
− cash out	5,000	3,000	3,000	8,000	4,000	4,000
= cash to carry forward	?	−1,000	?	−9,000	−1,000	?

6 In which month or months would the business have its biggest cash surplus?

(a) January

(b) February

(c) March

(d) April

(e) May

(f) June

7   Which THREE of the following would a business usually include in a business plan to be presented to a bank?

(a) a cash-flow forecast

(b) a description of the type of business and its market

(c) details of market research carried out on the market

(d) a catalogue to show what type of stock the business would be buying

(e) the letterhead and notepaper for the business

8   A business finds a new supplier for its raw materials. It now buys them 10% more cheaply. Which TWO of the following are the most likely effects on the business?

(a) the profit level will rise

(b) the profit level will fall

(c) prices to customers will fall

(d) costs will rise

(e) costs will fall

The next two questions are based on the following passage.

Jayne has always been a keen gardener and is thinking about opening a fruit and vegetable shop to sell her produce. She buys seeds and seedlings from a local garden centre and then raises the plants in her own garden. Her costs include the pots that she has to buy and the fertiliser she uses. She also has to spend a lot of time in the garden.

9   Which TWO of the following might be considered as Jayne's non-financial motivations for starting a business?

(a) profit

(b) independence

(c) expansion

(d) doing a job she enjoys

(e) growth

10 Which TWO of the following would be most likely to reduce the profits of Jayne's business?

(a) an increase in the price of seeds and seedlings

(b) better yields from her garden due to good weather

(c) a reduction in prices by competing local fruit and vegetable sellers

(d) a supermarket nearby deciding to stop selling fresh vegetables

(e) longer opening hours at the garden centre

Total: 20 marks

Topic 14

Customer needs and the marketing mix

What the specification requires

You need to understand that a business can only succeed if it can attract customers and keep them happy. It must therefore try to find out what customers might want (anticipate wants) and then meet those wants. Businesses will achieve this by using a combination of **product**, price, **promotion** and **place**. You should be able to recommend an appropriate mix for a smaller business, with a limited budget.

In brief

There are four key areas used to market any product once the business has found out what its customers want. These four parts of the 'marketing mix' — price, product, promotion and place — are often just known as the 'four Ps'.

It is important to remember that each part makes up just one-quarter of the marketing mix, and that it is most important for a business to get the balance right. It is no use having a fantastic product if no one knows about it, or if it can only be made at a price that no one is willing to pay.

Revision notes

- A business needs to find out what its customers want. It can then provide this. The business also needs to predict future needs so that it can plan for them.
- Market information can be gathered through market research.

- Customers' wants are met through the marketing mix — a balance of product, place, price and promotion.
- The product is the result of business activity. Without a product the business has nothing to sell. Products can be either goods or services. Goods can be touched and felt; services are 'invisible' and done for or to a person or organisation. Examples of personal services for individuals and groups are plumbing, entertainment, taxi rides and tourism. Examples of commercial services are insurance, retailing and transport.
- Price is the amount at which a business offers products for sale. The price of a product may be linked to a number of factors, including what it costs to produce, the price of competing products, the level of profit the business wants and the need for quick sales.

Speak the language

product — the good or service produced for sale

promotion — how a business tells customers that its product exists and tries to persuade them to buy

place — the place where a product is sold and how the product gets to that place

distribution — how the product gets to the customer or place where it is sold

e-commerce — buying and selling online

- Promotion consists of telling customers that a product exists and persuading them to buy it.
- Place covers both where a product can be bought and how it gets to that place. Finding the right place and **distribution** channels depends on the target market.
- **E-commerce** has opened up much wider markets, so that some products (such as music tracks) can now easily be distributed online. Small businesses can offer internet sales with a service where ordering online is backed up by home delivery using couriers or the postal service.
- Different businesses will have different emphases within their marketing mix, according to the wants of their customers. They will change the mix to respond to changing customer wants.

In a nutshell

* A business needs to find out what its customers want.
* It can the alter the marketing mix to make sure that they are happy.
* Product, price, promotion and place are the parts of the marketing mix.
* Product is the good or service for sale.
* Price is the amount at which a business offers a product for sale. Increases in price will affect demand, and fewer products will usually be sold (and vice versa).
* Businesses in competition have to be careful about changing price.
* Promotion tells customers about products and tries to sell them.
* Place is where a customer buys and delivery to that place.
* E-commerce has extended the market for small businesses.

AO1 to AO2: one way to boost your grade from AO1 to AO2 is to provide explanations. For example, you should be able to explain why a national television promotion campaign would be unsuitable for a small business. Key words like 'because' and 'as' show that you are explaining reasons.

Test yourself

Choose the most appropriate answer from each of the choices below.

1 The key information businesses need to find out about customers is **(a)** what they wear, **(b)** what they eat, **(c)** what they want, **(d)** where they live.

2 The product is the result of business **(a)** profits , **(b)** activity, **(c)** demand, **(d)** marketing.

3 A product that can be touched is called **(a)** a good, **(b)** a personal service, **(c)** a commercial service, **(d)** a range.

4 A product that is done to or for someone is called **(a)** a good, **(b)** a range, **(c)** a variety, **(d)** a service.

5 A business selling many products has a wide **(a)** demand, **(b)** price range, **(c)** product range, **(d)** number of customers.

6 A narrow product range leaves a business vulnerable to: **(a)** low prices, **(b)** taxation, **(c)** changes in the product, **(d)** changes in the market.

7 If prices fall, demand tends to **(a)** fall, **(b)** rise, **(c)** stay the same, **(d)** be worth more.

8 A business that increases prices could see a fall in all the following *except* **(a)** revenue, **(b)** profit, **(c)** demand, **(d)** product range.

9 Businesses tell customers about products through **(a)** prediction, **(b)** premonition, **(c)** promotion, **(d)** price.

10 'Place' as part of the marketing mix also covers **(a)** promotion, **(b)** marketing, **(c)** distribution, **(d)** price.

Topic 15
Choosing a legal structure

What the specification requires

You should know and understand that a small business, especially a start-up business, is limited to certain types of legal organisation. These are **sole trader**, **partnership** and **private limited company**. You need to understand what is meant by **limited liability** and how this can be of benefit to a business. You need to understand how increasing the number of stakeholders can bring both advantages and disadvantages.

In brief

Only certain types of legal structure are appropriate for a small business. The smallest is the 'one-person' business — the sole trader. Partnerships are agreements between two or more people to share the responsibilities and organisation of the business — and also to share workload and profits (or losses). Both of these have the drawback of unlimited **liability** for the owners. Private limited companies bring the owners the benefit of limiting their liability, but could also bring them problems by introducing more stakeholders, with different aims and objectives for the business.

Revision notes

- A start-up business could be a sole trader, partnership, private limited company or cooperative. It would not be a public limited company.
- Private limited companies have limited liability. This means that the responsibility for the debts of the business is limited to the amount that directors put in.
- This can be of benefit to the business's reputation, but banks may be reluctant to lend to small companies without guarantees. Extra stakeholders, such as shareholders, can also mean disagreements that hinder the efficient operation of the business.

Partnerships draw on the expertise and resources of more than one person

- A sole trader is a business that is owned and run by one person. The owner raises the finance him or herself, from personal sources (own funds) or by borrowing. The owner has sole control of the business, makes all the decisions and receives all of any profit. Sole traders gain from being independent. Raising more money is often hard, so expanding the business may be difficult.
- A partnership is a business that is owned by two or more people jointly.
- In sole traders and partnerships, owners are personally responsible for all the debts of the business. Each has unlimited liability. This means that owners are responsible for the debts of the business up to the whole extent that they are able to pay. This can be a huge risk. If the business is unable to pay its debts, personal assets (such as cars and houses) can be seized to pay them.

In a nutshell

* Start-up businesses will be established as sole traders, partnerships or private limited companies.
* Each legal type is suitable for a small business.
* Sole traders carry all the responsibility themselves, but gain all of any profit.
* Partners share both responsibility and profit.
* Private companies protect themselves by limiting liability.

Test yourself.

Try this short knowledge question.

George is an accountant, Harry is a chef. George and Harry wish to set up a catering business as a partnership. Explain two benefits to them of setting up as a partnership. *(4 marks)*

Boost your grade

AO1 to AO2: you will need to provide explanations and examples to move from AO1 to AO2. AO1 is usually 'give' or describe'. Always put your answer in context, by giving examples from businesses that you have studied.

Topic 16
Start-up legal and tax issues

What the specification requires

You should know that a business needs to establish itself with a unique and memorable name. You should understand why it is important for any business to keep complete and accurate records, both for its own planning and operation, and for bodies such as the taxation authorities.

In brief

All businesses have to start somewhere, and this is usually by finding a good name to go with the initial business idea. To start the business, certain formalities must be completed. For sole traders and partnerships these are few and uncomplicated, and involve making sure that they are paying correct amounts of tax and National Insurance. Private limited companies must be registered, have more complex regulations and pay different taxation.

Revision notes

- Sole traders and partnerships are easy and cheap to set up; no formal paperwork or registration is needed, although partnerships sometimes draw up a deed of partnership to make sure there are no misunderstandings. Sole traders and partners trade as themselves, so are liable to personal income tax. They are also responsible for paying **National Insurance** (this is the deduction that covers National Health Service healthcare and old-age pensions). They will need to fill in a tax return each year to ensure that income tax and appropriate National Insurance contributions have been paid.
- The accounts of sole traders and partnerships do not have to be made public. However, they do need to be accurate for HM Revenue and Customs.

All companies need to be registered with Companies House

- **Companies** have to be legally established and registered at Companies House. They must produce certain accounts, which are available to the public. They also have to inform the tax authorities of their existence and pay an income tax on the profits of the business (**corporation tax**). If turnover is large enough, the business must also register for **VAT**.
- Every business needs to find a unique and memorable name which can be registered to protect it.
- Businesses have a legal responsibility to keep careful records to ensure that they meet their responsibilities regarding taxation (such as income tax, corporation tax and VAT) and National Insurance for everyone concerned with the business — not just the owners, but also the employees.

In a nutshell

* Start-up businesses need a unique and memorable name.
* They will be established as sole traders, partnerships or private limited companies.
* Each has legal obligations once set up.
* Sole traders and partners must keep careful records so that they pay the right tax and National Insurance.
* Private limited companies must register with Companies House and will pay corporation tax on profits.
* Any business with employees has further legal duties towards them.

Test yourself

Give short answers to the following questions.

1 Define the following forms of deduction from a typical wage packet:
   (a) income tax
   (b) National Insurance contribution

2 Outline the responsibilities of companies as regards:
   (a) records
   (b) taxation

3 Outline the paperwork that must be completed by sole traders and partnerships.

Boost your grade

AO1 to AO2: you will find it easier to describe the various tax and other obligations of a start-up business if you use a real business example with which you are familiar.

Topic 17
Customer satisfaction

What the specification requires

You need to understand that the survival and success of small businesses may depend on levels of customer satisfaction. Satisfied customers will both return to make repeat purchases and recommend the business to other potential customers. Dissatisfied customers will persuade people not to use a business. Satisfaction comes from reliable service, clear product information and good after-sales service.

In brief

Customer service is used to attract customers and, more importantly, to keep them by ensuring that customers are satisfied. It is much cheaper for a business to retain customers than it is for the business to try to win new ones. Good customer service is key to a business retaining customers. Customers expect orders to be met on time and accurately, to be given good information and advice, and to have good **after-sales service** available, such as good complaints and returns policies. New technology has opened up new ways to keep customers happy, such as via web ordering.

Revision notes

- Good customer service leading to customer satisfaction is vital to the success of small businesses.
- A key part of customer service is reliability. For example, shops are expected to be open at the times they state, tradespeople to visit when they say they will, and products to perform to a high standard.
- Customers also rely on accurate information, which must provide, as a minimum, what the law asks: for example, safe use of a product. Information and advice given about a product must be accurate, even if it is verbal. Customers should expect specialist advice if they ask a retail assistant about a product. Staff should be trained to give correct advice.

Customers don't like to be kept hanging on

- After-sales service may sometimes be as important as the product. For example, if you bought a car but then found that spare parts for it were unavailable, the car would be useless. In some cases, after-sales service includes guarantees. Sometimes service extends for years; in other cases, it may involve nothing more than a delivery service, or the wrapping of the product. After-sales service also involves dealing with complaints, refunds and exchanges.
- Complaints should be dealt with properly and professionally — the customer may then be retained.
- Retaining customers is vital to success. Without repeat sales to existing customers, many businesses would fail. By building customer loyalty, a business can benefit from the **lifetime sales** of a customer. Imagine how much you would spend in your life at the same shops if you always used the same ones. This is what businesses aim to achieve by keeping customers happy.

Speak the language

customer service — looking after customers so as to attract and retain them

after-sales service — the part of customer service that takes place after a sale is made

lifetime sales — the amount a customer will spend over a lifetime on a particular type of good or service

In a nutshell

* Good customer service is a key factor for small businesses in creating customer satisfaction.
* Customer satisfaction is linked to reliability, quality and after-sales service.
* Retaining customers is cheaper than finding new ones.
* Businesses are keen to keep customers satisfied so as to retain them.

Test yourself

Customers require information, advice, after-sales service and different ways to pay before they are satisfied. Draw up a table with these headings and list the terms below under the appropriate heading (some may apply to more than one area).

Information	Advice	After-sales	Ways to pay

accurate   as required   cards   cash

clear   credit   delivery   guarantees

helpful   packaging   specialist

Boost your grade

AO1 to AO2: for some businesses, different aspects of customer service are going to be more or less important in encouraging customer satisfaction. AO2 marks often depend on you using an example to explain an answer, so you should choose the right types of customer service to recommend, depending on the business you are discussing.

Topic 18
Recruiting, training and motivating staff

You should know that small businesses may also be employers, so they will recruit, train and motivate workers. You should understand that workers have a right to decent and safe working conditions and fair pay for the work they undertake. Employers have the right to expect employees to be punctual, efficient and loyal, and have the responsibility to provide good working conditions and fair pay.

In brief

Businesses may need both full-time and part-time employees. They will pay employees according to their qualities, such as skill and experience. Employees may also gain other benefits, such as pensions and bonuses. **Motivation** means that employees work because they want to, generally because they can see a benefit from the action. In a business, a motivated worker will work harder, better and more effectively. There are laws in the area of employment rights, including health and safety, discrimination, equal pay and minimum wages.

Revision notes

- **Recruitment** is the process by which a business finds new employees. Even a small business, such as a sole trader, may need to recruit employees. Sometimes staff are taken on because they have been recommended. Usually appointment follows a process.
- The selection process usually starts with an advertisement. Applicants' **CVs** and letters of support are read. Shortlisted applicants are invited to interview. Interviews in a small business are likely to be one-to-one. They could involve tests to show that the candidate can really do the job. After the interviews, the best candidate is offered the job.

An interview panel

- Employers look at both the skills and experience they need and the enthusiasm and attitude of a candidate. The candidate who seems better motivated will often gain the job over the one that is better qualified.
- All businesses benefit from motivated staff. Motivation means people working more effectively because they want to, and is sometimes linked to a reward. Businesses use many ways to motivate. Some are financial, such as bonuses or profit-sharing; some are non-financial, such as praise and promotion, or supporting staff in training or education.
- Small businesses may offer motivation linked to their market. A shop could offer a reward for sales; a service outlet could reward on the basis of customer feedback.

- Employees have the right to fair treatment. The law states that in all matters of recruitment, selection, training and promotion, there should be no **discrimination** on grounds of gender, race, religion, creed, sexual orientation, disability or age. This includes the right to equal pay for equal work or responsibility.

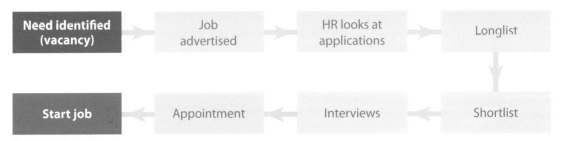

The recruitment process

In a nutshell

* Even the smallest businesses may need employees.
* The recruitment process may be informal (e.g. by recommendation) or a formal process from job advertisement through interview to appointment.
* Businesses balance qualifications against motivation when recruiting.
* Businesses use a variety of ways to motivate because motivated workers are better and more efficient at their jobs.
* Employees have the right to fair and equal treatment.

Test yourself

Match the term or phrase on the left with the most suitable term on the right. The terms on the right show ways to motivate or rewards from motivation.

1	financial	status
2	further a career	training
3	maximum sales	extra sales
4	more responsibility	customer feedback
5	non-financial	profit-sharing
6	retail outlet	promotion
7	service outlet	praise
8	status	prize

AO1: you should think about how an employer can show that it is being fair, and treating people equally, as this is what the law is based on. Any unfair or unequal treatment (such as discrimination) is likely to be against the law.

Section test: Making the start-up effective

Jez has started a business with his friend Steve. They noticed that many colleges and universities had their own scarves and T-shirts, with the name and logo of the institution. They though that school sixth-formers would like to buy the same sort of items, but much more fashionably produced. They are producing and selling wide belts (a current fashion craze) with school logos worked into the leather. They carried out market research and were pleased to find that their idea would be a success.

1   Which of these is the key information that Jez and Steve needed to find out about customers through their market research?
   (a) what they wear   (c) what they want
   (b) what they eat   (d) where they live

2   The belts that they produce would be best described as which of the following?
   (a) a good   (d) a range
   (b) a personal service   (e) raw materials
   (c) a commercial service

3   Steve and Jez's business might be considered to be vulnerable because it has which of the following?
   (a) a narrow product range   (d) good advertising
   (b) good levels of demand   (e) a unique product
   (c) low production costs

4   Steve and Jez are thinking of charging higher prices. This could mean that they could see a fall in all of the following EXCEPT
   (a) revenue   (d) product range
   (b) profit   (e) hours worked by the friends
   (c) demand

5 Steve and Jez have discussed the type of legal structure they want for their business. Jez favours a private limited company. Which TWO of the following might be the most likely reasons for this preference?
   (a) He wants to reduce the risk of personal loss.
   (b) He wants to be the only owner of the business.
   (c) He would have access to unlimited sources of finance.
   (d) He wants to raise large amounts of money on the stock exchange.
   (e) He would only be liable for the amount he invested if the business failed.

6 Choose TWO of the following as good reasons why good customer service is important to the success of this business.
   (a) It is a legal requirement.
   (b) It has a unique product.
   (c) Customers will tell their friends about good service.
   (d) Customers are the ones who add value.
   (e) A small business needs customers to return for repeat purchases.

7 Which of the following would be the TWO most likely reasons why Jez and Steve have to keep careful records of the income and expenditure of the business?
   (a) so their accountant has the right information
   (b) in case any staff were stealing from the business
   (c) to make sure they are paying the right levels of tax
   (d) to make sure they are paying the right levels of National Insurance
   (e) to show to the bank manager

8 What would be the TWO most likely effects of an unexpected rise in the demand for Jez and Steve's belts?
   (a) Their profits would fall.
   (b) Fewer people might buy the belts.
   (c) There might be too many belts on the market.
   (d) There might be too few belts on the market.
   (e) The price of the belts would be likely to rise.

9 Which of the following is not covered by discrimination law?
   (a) gender   (d) disability
   (b) politics   (e) race
   (c) age

10 Steve and Jez need to compete with a larger business that is producing similar goods. Suggest which TWO of the following actions would be the best to take.
   (a) Lowering their prices below those of the competitor.
   (b) Launching an advertising campaign on national television.
   (c) Providing an ordering service for hard-to-find CDs for their customers.
   (d) Opening up two new stores in the town.
   (e) Focusing on improving the quality of customer service.

Topic 19
Small businesses and commodity prices

What the specification requires

You need to understand what the term **commodities** means and why commodities are important to small businesses. You need to know how the prices set on commodity markets can have an impact on small businesses and that this, in turn, can affect the prices that businesses charge their customers.

In brief

Commodities are major crop and raw-material products that are bought in bulk and similar wherever they are produced. Although their price is set by the operation of supply and demand, there are other complicating factors in commodity markets. Demand is not just for now, but for the future. Supply is slow and difficult to change. Prices are also affected by traders gambling on future price changes. Commodity prices cannot be influenced by small businesses, but changes in them can have a large effect on such businesses.

Revision notes

- Commodities are products such as crops and raw materials that are basically the same wherever they are produced (copper from China is no different from copper from Russia, or Brazil). Examples are wheat, barley, rice, copper, coffee, oil, sugar, aluminium, iron ore, steel, and other metals and ores.
- Commodities are bought and sold in huge amounts, in **organised markets** — that is, markets conducted according to strict trading rules. There are many supply-and-demand factors that affect the price. Prices arc set by the interaction of buyers (demand) and producers (supply) in international markets.
- Buyers will either be working on behalf of large companies that wish to buy in huge amounts — such as building

Wheat is a commodity

companies, telecoms firms and cereal manufacturers — or buying as a gamble on future prices (speculating). The large companies must have the commodity or they will not be able to continue trading, so they will be keen to ensure supply for future years by also buying for delivery in the future.

- Supply comes from mining and extraction companies and agricultural producers. Although there may be many producers, there will still be a single world price for a commodity.
- Commodity markets are slow to change — it is difficult to increase the supply of wheat, or coffee, or aluminium, except in the long term — and prices are also affected by speculation, so these are not like normal markets.
- However, commodity prices are still important to many small businesses — bakers are affected by wheat prices, plumbers by copper prices, petrol stations by oil prices.
- Small businesses may also struggle if there are increases in fuel and energy prices. These are linked to the prices of raw materials, as they are dependent on commodities such as oil, gas and coal.

In a nutshell

* Commodities are raw materials and similar goods.
* Their prices are decided on international markets.
* Many large businesses have to ensure that they have a supply of key commodities.
* Commodity prices also affect many small businesses.

Speak the language

commodities — raw material or energy products that are the same wherever they are produced

organised markets — international markets that trade according to strict rules

Test yourself

Boost your grade

Fill in the missing words from the list below. If you are feeling confident, cover the words and do the exercise from memory.

Commodities are products like .... and .... that are basically the same wherever they are produced. Supply comes from .... and .... companies and .... producers. Although there may be many producers, there will still be a single world .... for a commodity. .... comes mostly from large businesses that need to buy in huge amounts. These businesses must have the commodity or they will not be able to continue trading. For example, a cereal manufacturer must have supplies of wheat, barley and sugar. .... are set by the interaction of demand and .... in .... markets.

AO2 to AO3: if you can talk about how prices of commodities are set on international markets, yet can have a big effect on the profits and even survival of small businesses, you will be discussing an effect in detail, so will be working at AO3. You may have the chance to do this in your controlled assessment.

(agricultural) (crops) (demand) (extraction) (international)
(mining) (price) (prices) (raw materials) (supply)

GCSE Revision Guide

Topic 20
External economic influences: interest and exchange rates

What the specification requires

You need to understand that there are many economic influences over which small businesses have no control. These will be more or less significant to the business depending on the nature of the business. For some businesses, changes in exchange rates may be important; for other businesses, they will have little effect. You will need to know how to calculate changes in exchange rates.

In brief

External influences are those that are outside the control of a business. They include major economic factors such as changes in interest rates, changes in foreign exchange rates and the economic cycles that give rise to consumer booms and downturns, which can become recessions. Many businesses, both small and large, are influenced by such changes, sometimes favourably, sometimes not. The extent of the influence will be strongly linked to the type of market in which the business trades.

Revision notes

- **Interest rates** are the price of borrowing money. In the UK, they are set centrally by the Bank of England. If interest rates are high, or increase, this makes it more expensive to borrow money. This has an effect on both businesses and consumers.
- Businesses, particularly small ones that rely on overdrafts, bank loans and good credit terms with suppliers, will find it more expensive to borrow if interest rates rise. They may not be able to hold as much stock, or as wide a range as they would want to. They may also not be able to offer credit terms to customers. Higher interest rates also reduce consumer spending.
- **Exchange rates** are the value of a particular currency (e.g. for the UK, the pound sterling, £) in terms of other currencies (e.g. the US dollar, $, or the EU euro, €). Businesses trading internationally will have to buy

The price of goods imported or exported is affected by currency exchange rates or sell in a foreign currency. If a UK business imports a product from an EU country, it will have to pay in euros, so at some point a £/€ conversion takes place. The value of the pound will fluctuate depending on many factors such as the strength of the economy and interest rates. A higher pound means cheaper imports and more expensive exports (and vice versa). For example, at an exchange rate of £1 = €2, a £100 export sells for €200. If the exchange rate falls to £1 = €1.5, the £100 export is now worth only €150.

In a nutshell

* Some influences are outside the control of the business.
* These are called external factors.
* One is the price of borrowing money — interest rates.
* One is the price of other currencies — foreign exchange rates.
* Changes in either of these can have an effect on a small business.
* The size of the effect depends on the market in which the business operates.

Test yourself

Calculate the price in US dollars, euros or sterling of each of the following, as appropriate. Assume that the exchange rates are £1 = €1.1 and £1 = $1.6.

1 A UK business buys £1,000 worth of fruit from France.
   (a) Will payment be made in dollars, pounds or euros?
   (b) What is the amount to pay?

2 An American car manufacturer sells £150,000 worth of cars to a garage in London.
   (a) Will the garage make payment in dollars, pounds or euros?
   (b) What is the amount to pay?

3 An Italian tourist buys a holiday in the Lake District in northern England. It is priced in Italy at €750.
   (a) Will payment to the holiday company be made in dollars, pounds or euros?
   (b) What is the amount to pay?

4 A UK business buys £20,000 worth of wheat from the USA.
   (a) Will payment be made in dollars, pounds or euros?
   (b) What is the amount to pay?

5 A German business needs payment for £3,000 worth of parts sold to a Birmingham car company.
   (a) Will payment be made in dollars, pounds or euros?
   (b) What is the amount to pay?

Boost your grade

AO1: you may be asked to do simple calculations with regard to exchange rates. You should always check these carefully to make sure, first, that you have gone in the right direction (dollar to pound, or pound to dollar, for example) and secondly, that you have the decimal point in the right place.

Topic 21
External economic influences: business cycles

What the specification requires

You should know that the economy tends to rise and fall in cycles, with periods of growth followed by periods of **recession**. You need to understand that small businesses are affected by business cycles, and may be more vulnerable to such changes than larger businesses.

In brief

Changes to the economy tend to happen in cycles that go from 'boom' to 'bust' to 'boom' again, and so on, via 'recession' and 'recovery'. Changes in **economic activity** are used to chart the cycles. When economic activity (i.e. output and demand) is on the increase, businesses find it easier to survive, succeed and become profitable. When economic activity is falling, many small businesses will find it hard to survive and may only manage to do so by cutting back on costs, such as staff costs.

Revision notes

- Economic activity tends to go in cycles that are reckoned to last between 8 and 10 years.
- Cycles go from years of boom, through downturns called recessions, and then on to upturns or recovery.
- Boom years have high levels of consumer spending and low levels of unemployment. However, at the top of the boom, there will be rising wages and rising prices. Businesses will find it harder and harder to meet increased demand, which is what pushes prices up.
- During a recession, demand falls (possibly as a result of higher prices and higher interest rates), and there is lower spending and high levels of unemployment. Businesses may find it harder to borrow money; this can be a particular problem for small businesses.

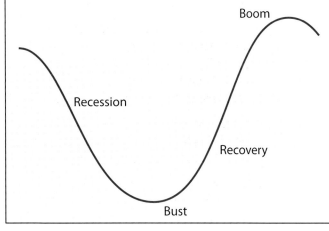

The business cycle

- Levels of **economic growth** signal whether an economy is heading for boom or recession. Economic growth is measured by output and expenditure in an economy. Positive growth means strong demand. This is good for small businesses.
- Negative or zero growth means weak demand. This is bad for small businesses, which may struggle to survive.
- Small businesses are likely to be more vulnerable and the first to be badly affected by a recession. However, the effect on a business depends on the type of business. Those selling luxury products and services that people can easily do without, such as foreign holidays, are likely to suffer most.

Speak the language

recession — when growth is either zero or negative for a period of time

economic activity — charts the levels of demand and output in the economy as a whole

economic growth — increases in output and demand in the economy

In a nutshell

* The economy goes through periods of rise and fall.
* This is measured through economic activity, such as demand.
* When demand is growing, businesses find it easier to do well.
* When demand falls, many small businesses find it hard to survive.
* Most likely to be affected are those businesses selling products that people can easily do without.

Boost your grade

AO1 to AO2: for basic marks you should be able to describe how a business might suffer in an economic downturn. You are not expected to know specific terms used in business cycles, such as 'recession', but will gain AO2 marks if you can use them to show better understanding in the context of an answer, perhaps as part of a controlled assessment.

Test yourself

Match the term or phrase on the left with the most appropriate term or phrase on the right.

1	boom	recession
2	downturn	recovery
3	high unemployment	high consumer spending
4	rising wages and prices	bottom of a cycle
5	upturn	top of a cycle

Topic 22
The influence on stakeholders

What the specification requires

You need to know what is meant by the term **stakeholder** in connection with business. You need to understand that stakeholders can both be influenced by the actions of a business, and also have an influence on the actions of a business. In particular, you should understand how stakeholders can influence small businesses.

In brief

Businesses can exist only if people take risks on new products or ideas, or in new markets. The owners of the business are usually the ones who carry most of the risk. They obviously have a stake in how well the business succeeds. Once a business exists there will be many people, other than the owners, who have an interest in its success (or failure). Stakeholders are those people, groups or organisations that have a stake in a business.

Revision notes

- Stakeholders with a direct interest in the business are called **internal stakeholders** and they include owners and employees. In a small business the owner will be a single person (sole trader), or a small group of people (partnerships, cooperatives, private limited companies).
- **Shareholders** are a special group of owners. Each has a share of the business. In private limited companies, shareholders are limited to family and friends.
- Owners would like success and profit. They can influence a business by investing. Owners make key decisions about the business, such as what to sell, what markets to operate in and whether to expand.

- Employees would like decent working conditions and fair pay. Employees can influence the business through working hard and being skilled and motivated — or not.
- Managers are the employees who help run the business. Their influence extends to taking day-to-day decisions in the business.
- **External stakeholders** have a less direct stake in a business. They include customers, suppliers, banks, communities, government and pressure groups.
- Customers want quality and reliability. They influence the business by buying or not.
- Suppliers influence the business through quality and reliability of supply.
- Financial stakeholders, such as banks, have lent or given the business money. They can take decisions that are in their own interests, rather than those of the business.
- The community may want the business for some reasons (e.g. employment) but not others (e.g. pollution).
- Government influences business through laws and taxation.
- Pressure groups try to influence businesses to bring about change.

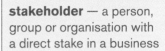

Speak the language

stakeholder — a person, group or organisation with a direct stake in a business

internal stakeholders — those with a direct interest in a business

shareholders — owners of shares in a business (all shareholders are stakeholders but not vice versa)

external stakeholders — individuals, groups or other businesses that have a less direct stake in a business.

In a nutshell

- * All businesses have stakeholders.
- * Internal stakeholders have a direct stake.
- * They can influence the business through the way they work and make decisions.
- * External stakeholders have a more indirect stake.
- * They can have a lot of influence on a small business: for example, customers not buying, suppliers not supplying good-quality inputs, or governments setting tax too high.

Boost your grade

AO1 to AO2: sometimes stakeholder groups have conflicting aims. For example, customers may want lower prices, while shareholders want higher profits; suppliers may want paying immediately, while the business wants to delay payment; a business may want to expand operations and the community wants to keep it small. You may be asked to look at both sides of an argument and then be asked to make a decision. Always use the business example to help you, if one is given.

Test yourself

Try this exam-style question.

Angie owns a drive-in burger bar. It normally shuts at 10 p.m. As the local cinema has decided to stay open until midnight, Angie has decided to extend her opening hours. She is in a residential district and local people have complained about late-night traffic noise. They have appealed to the local council to restrict the burger bar to 10 p.m. closing.

1 Identify TWO stakeholders in this situation.   *(2 marks)*

2 Select TWO stakeholders and explain how their aims conflict.   *(3 marks)*

3 Advise the council whether or not to uphold the appeal.   *(7 marks)*

Section test: Understanding the economic context

1 Which TWO of the following breakfast items are most likely to be 'commodities'?
   (a) sugar   (d) eggs
   (b) milk   (e) bacon
   (c) coffee

2 Commodity prices are decided on international markets through which TWO of the following?
   (a) the interaction of buyers and prices
   (b) speculators buying because they think that the price will change
   (c) the interaction of buyers and sellers
   (d) the operation of supply and demand
   (e) the interaction of suppliers and producers

3 Commodity prices may be important to small businesses because
   (a) small business people need a good breakfast
   (b) many use commodities in their work
   (c) small businesses operate internationally
   (d) small businesses want to grow
   (e) all businesses are affected to the same extent by changes in price

4 If an American entrepreneur decided to open a branch of his Japanese restaurant chain in England, in which currency would the branch have to pay its UK employees?
   (a) US dollars   (d) Canadian dollars
   (b) European Union euros   (e) Japanese yen
   (c) UK pounds sterling

5 If a French tourist buys a holiday in Blackpool and pays €600 for it, and the exchange rate is €1 = 90p, what amount will the holiday company receive?
   (a) €540
   (b) €600
   (c) £540
   (d) £600
   (e) £666

6 If the exchange rate changed to €1 = 80p, the price to pay would now be
   (a) £540 or €600
   (b) €600 or £480
   (c) £540 or €540
   (d) £600 or €600
   (e) £540 or €480

7 The exchange-rate change would be which THREE of the following?
   (a) of benefit to the exporter
   (b) of benefit to the importer
   (c) a disadvantage to the exporter
   (d) a disadvantage to the importer
   (e) an advantage to the tourist

The next three questions are based on the passage that follows. Read the passage and answer the questions.

Marshall's imports top-of-the-range sports cars from Italy. Many of its customers take out loans in order to buy the cars and Marshall's works with a credit company to provide these. Recently, one of the importer's specialist car-cleaning machines broke down and it had to spend £10,000 on buying a new one from its American suppliers.

8 If interest rates rose in the UK, which TWO of the following are the most likely effects on the business?
   (a) The business would not be affected because it had no savings.
   (b) The business would see a fall in demand.
   (c) The business would see its costs falling.
   (d) The business would see its sales slow down.
   (e) The business would see an increase in demand.

9 If the exchange rate between the US dollar and the pound sterling was $1 = 65p, how much would Marshall's have to pay for its machine?
   (a) £15,384
   (b) $15,384
   (c) €15,384
   (d) £6,500
   (e) $6,500

10 Which of the following might NOT be considered to be stakeholders in Marshall's?
   (a) its owners, the Marshall family
   (b) the American supplier from which it bought the machine
   (c) Italian sports car manufacturers
   (d) the government of Italy
   (e) Italian pasta makers

·Practice exam

Edexcel paper 1 is 45 minutes long and contains various types of multiple-choice and short-answer questions. You are advised to attempt to answer each question, and to return to questions that you have not answered at the end of the paper if you have time.

Questions 1–5 are based on the passage that follows. Read the passage and answer the questions.

Leonardo Kocapelli has set up an organic ice cream business, producing exotic flavours of ice cream. He makes these in a small unit on an industrial estate and sells them to local restaurants and through farm shops. Before setting up, he checked to see if any other businesses were providing the same product, but found that his flavours were unique. Leonardo set up on his own, although he could have become a franchisee for Tony Romes Ices. This would have given him a bigger market.

1 **Kocapelli's is a new business. Leonardo needed to analyse the strengths and weaknesses of possible competitors because**
   (a) he needs to employ people
   (b) he will be able to compete more effectively
   (c) he is on an industrial estate
   (d) he has internet access
   (e) he sells organic produce   *(1 mark)*

2 **Leonardo thinks that being organic adds value to his product. Adding value to a product means that a customer receives which of the following?**
   (a) competitor value   **(d)** better service
   (b) more value for money   **(e)** better ice cream
   (c) more products   *(1 mark)*

3 **Leonardo delivers to his customers and always tries to be on time. Why is customer service important to the success of small businesses?**
   (a) because the government says so
   (b) because customers add value
   (c) because small businesses need loyalty
   (d) because they sell many products
   (e) because they have to obey the law   *(1 mark)*

4 **Leonardo decided not to become a franchisee. A franchisee is**
   (a) the seller of the franchise
   (b) the buyer of the franchise
   (c) the owner of the brand
   (d) a customer of the franchise
   (e) a competitor of the franchise   *(1 mark)*

5 **Leonardo paid for his machinery so he would be able to start producing. He also bought a van for deliveries. The costs he paid once, when Kocapelli's was first established, are called**

(a) start-up costs

(b) set-up costs

(c) beginning costs

(d) establishment costs

(e) machinery costs

(1 mark)

6 **Consider the statements below referring to sole traders and limited companies.**

Sole trader	Limited company
■ Owns all the business	■ Shares ownership
■ Keeps all the profit	■ Shares profit
■ Is liable for all the losses	■ Shares liability
■ Could lose personal possessions	■ Has limited liability
■ Takes all the decisions	■ Shares decision-making

A start-up business that wanted to minimise its risks would be advised to choose which legal format?

(a) sole trader

(b) limited company

(1 mark)

Questions 7–10 are based on the passage that follows. Read the passage and answer the questions.

Misbah works for a small business in the north of England. The business makes and exports children's toys. Misbah sometimes has to work late and, when an order needs completing, even on Saturdays. She is a hard worker but feels that she is not always appreciated as much as she could be. Recently, she has had an idea for a new type of children's toy, and feels she could develop it herself.

7 **Which THREE of the following are the most likely reasons why Misbah might want to start a business?**

(a) to make a profit

(b) to work as little as possible

(c) to achieve an ambition

(d) to make sure she has an easy life

(e) to be independent

(3 marks)

8 **Which one of the following does Misbah have that is an important skill for an entrepreneur?**

(a) not being worried about risk

(b) employing at least five workers

(c) a willingness to work hard

(d) a willingness to study business studies

(e) the ability to raise finance

(1 mark)

9 **New businesses are often at risk of failure. Which TWO of the following would be considered a risk by a new business set-up, like Misbah's?**

(a) lack of demand
(b) lack of competition
(c) thorough market research
(d) staff who are not experienced
(e) detailed knowledge of the market

(2 marks)

10 **If Misbah decides to start her business, how can she reduce the risk of it failing? Choose THREE of the following.**

(a) starting it quickly
(b) forward planning
(c) having a unique product
(d) good research
(e) taking big risks

(3 marks)

Questions 11–13 are based on the passage and table that follow. Read the passage and table and answer the questions.

Brotherton's is a small business selling expensive holidays. It advertises as selling 'holidays of a lifetime' and many couples use their savings or take out loans for holidays for special occasions. Below is the cash-flow forecast for Brotherton's for the last 6 months of 2010 (£000s).

	July	August	September	October	November	December
RECEIPTS						
Revenue from sales	90	80	75	65	80	160
PAYMENTS						
Wages and salaries	20	20	?	20	20	20
Materials	20	20	20	20	30	?
Power and maintenance	10	5	5	10	10	10
Rent	20	20	20	20	20	20
Transport	10	10	5	5	5	10
Advertising	15	10	10	5	10	30
Total payments	95	85	80	80	95	120
Net cash flow	?	−5	−5	−15	−15	40
Opening balance	25	20	15	10	−5	?
Closing balance	20	15	10	−5	−20	20

Edexcel Business Studies

71

11 Calculate the missing figures. *(4 marks)*

12 In which month do you think Brotherton's will have to borrow the most?
    (a) July   **(d)** October
    (b) August   **(e)** November
    (c) September   **(f)** December   *(1 mark)*

13 If interest rates rose in the UK, which TWO of the following are the most likely effects on Brotherton's business?
    (a) The business would not be affected because it had no savings.
    (b) The business would see a fall in demand.
    (c) The business would see its costs falling.
    (d) The business would see its sales slow down.
    (e) The business would see an increase in demand.   *(2 marks)*

Questions 14–17 are based on the passage that follows. Read the passage and answer the questions.

George and Ali have planned their new business venture. They have £10,000 each to put into the business. They intend to start a business washing and valeting cars. They have made sure that there is a market for their product. They still have several items to buy before they can start trading. They need to buy a large machine to wash the cars, which will cost £40,000. They also need supplies of detergent and polish, and to pay the initial 6 months' rent on the premises they have chosen.

14 Which source of finance would George and Ali be most likely to use to buy the machine?
    (a) owners' funds   **(d)** trade credit
    (b) bank loan   **(e)** overdraft
    (c) mortgage   *(1 mark)*

15 Which source of finance would George and Ali consider if they were buying their premises for £100,000 rather than renting?
    (a) owners' funds   **(d)** trade credit
    (b) bank loan   **(e)** overdraft
    (c) mortgage   *(1 mark)*

16 If George and Ali did not want to use their own money at this stage, which source of finance would be best for monthly supplies of detergent and polish?
    (a) owners' funds   **(d)** trade credit
    (b) bank loan   **(e)** overdraft
    (c) mortgage   *(1 mark)*

17 George and Ali have discussed the type of legal structure they want for their business. Ali would prefer it if they set up a private limited company. Which TWO of the following might be the most likely reasons for this preference?

(a) He wants to reduce the risk of personal loss.

(b) He wants to be the only owner of the business.

(c) He would have access to unlimited sources of finance.

(d) He wants to raise large amounts of money on the stock exchange.

(e) If the business failed, he would only be liable for the amount he invested.　　*(2 marks)*

18 **TWO pieces of key information that George and Ali needed to find out about customers through their market research were:**

(a) what they would pay for the service

(b) how long they would wait while their cars were washed

(c) what sort of cars would come

(d) where their customers were driving from

(e) how many miles they drove a week　　*(2 marks)*

19 **George and Ali's business provides a single service — cleaning and polishing cars. This is a narrow product range, so would lead to their business**

(a) failing

(b) succeeding

(c) having many customers

(d) being vulnerable to market changes

(e) being immune to market changes　　*(1 mark)*

20 **Match the definition on the right with the correct term on the left. There is only one correct definition for each term.**

(a)	discrimination	those who take the risk of starting a business
(b)	entrepreneurs	the surplus of revenue over costs
(c)	fixed costs	approaching a problem from a different, often unusual, direction
(d)	promotion	where there is demand for a product but no product yet exists to fulfil that demand
(e)	lateral thinking	targets that are not money-related, like satisfaction and independence
(f)	limited liability	those costs that do not vary with production, like rent
(g)	non-financial objectives	how a business tells customers that its product exists and tries to persuade them to buy
(h)	profit	when liability is limited to the amount a shareholder invested
(i)	recession	acting unfairly towards someone because of something over which that person has no control
(j)	gap in the market	when growth is either zero or negative for a period of time

(10 marks)

TOTAL: 40 marks

Unit 3
Building a business

Topic 23

Marketing and market research

What the specification requires

You should realise that marketing is about understanding what it is that customers want, not just about selling. **Market research** is the way that businesses find out what customers want. Many methods of market research are either too expensive or too difficult for a small business to carry out. Larger businesses are often in a position to obtain better research.

In brief

Businesses need to collect information to help them to sell products to their customers. They need to know which group of customers might buy the product, how much they might be willing to spend, how often they will buy and what is attracting them to the product — why they want to buy. Businesses can find out this information through various means, such as asking questions or looking at market data. With this information the business can decide not only what to sell, but also how to change a product or develop new products to attract customers.

Questionnaires are one way for a business to gather information

Revision notes

- Market research involves the collection, collation, analysis and interpretation of data regarding a particular market.
- Such research may involve both **primary (field) research** and **secondary (desk) research**.
- Primary research is information that has not been collected before; it is 'first-hand' information. Often the methods of collecting primary research make it expensive, but it can be targeted and focused to collect exactly the data required.
- Secondary research is research that has been previously published. There are very good sources of secondary data, such as government statistics, and many less reliable sources,

such as the internet. Secondary research may be cheap (it may even be free — many government-collected statistics are available on the government website at www.statistics.gov.uk), but much of it will not fulfil the exact requirements of the business.

- It is part of the marketing function to ensure that there is a good balance of primary and secondary sources. There is science behind asking the right questions or researching the right secondary information, which often requires specialist researchers to produce the best results.
- Research may produce **quantitative** and **qualitative data** that have to be interpreted and analysed to be of use to a business.
- Quantitative data involve numbers and statistics and will, for example, show trends.
- Qualitative data involve opinions, views and interpretations, so may give deeper insights, but will be harder to analyse. Small groups of people called focus groups may be used to give opinions.
- Data are no use until they are interpreted. They then become 'information' and can be fed into the marketing mix.

Desk and field research compared

	Advantages	Disadvantages
Field research	■ Up to date ■ Targeted	■ Expensive ■ Time consuming ■ Large surveys needed for accuracy
Desk research	■ Cheap, even free ■ Easy to obtain	■ Out of date ■ Not exactly what is wanted ■ Some can be expensive

Desk research is cheap but it may be out of date

In a nutshell

* The main types of research are field/primary research and desk/secondary research.
* Field research is more reliable, but time-consuming and expensive.
* Desk research is cheap — often free — but may be out of date or unreliable.
* Both quantitative and qualitative data are important.
* Data need to be interpreted to become information; this can then be used to support the choice of marketing mix.

Boost your grade   **AO2 to AO3:** when presented with market research data, always ask yourself how valid it is. Look at the source and date. If you do not have raw data, but an opinion, this could be less reliable. For AO3 marks, use these arguments to support your analysis of data and as the reasons to support your judgements.

Test yourself

Choose the most appropriate answer from each of the choices below.

1 Market research is usually divided into desk research and **(a)** open research, **(b)** field research, **(c)** closed research, **(d)** concentrated research.

2 The two main types of research are also known as: **(a)** primary and tertiary, **(b)** secondary and tertiary, **(c)** primary and secondary, **(d)** outside and inside.

3 A small group asked for an opinion on a product is called **(a)** a focus group, **(b)** a delta group, **(c)** observation, **(d)** market data.

4 Company reports can be useful because they are easy to obtain and **(a)** free, **(b)** complicated, **(c)** online, **(d)** expensive.

5 The internet is a source that often provides free information. The main problem with this information is that it is not always **(a)** reliable, **(b)** easy to read **(c)** searchable, **(d)** in English.

Topic 24
Building a successful marketing mix: product

What the specification requires

You should understand that, as a business grows, it may wish to expand its **product portfolio**. You should know that, as the demand for a good or service changes over time, there is a natural 'life cycle' and that businesses may try to extend this life cycle.

In brief

Businesses use different techniques at the launch phase of a product to persuade customers to try it. Product trial may involve special offers and promotions. Once a customer has tried (and likes) a product, the business then aims to encourage repeat purchase. This means using techniques such as loyalty cards to bring repeat business. Such techniques are used at different stages of the product life cycle. The Boston matrix (see Topic 25) can be used to analyse the product portfolio of a business.

Revision notes

- Businesses need to persuade customers to try a new product. They also want repeat sales. Different marketing techniques are used to achieve these two outcomes.
- The **product life cycle** (see the diagram and table overleaf) shows the usual stages through which a product passes. Like a person, a product is born, grows old, matures and eventually dies. Some life cycles are very short, or explosive. Others are very long or extended. The stage of the life cycle is important to a business. It shows it what sort of promotion or other changes might be needed to boost sales.

Sainsbury's 'Taste the difference' product range

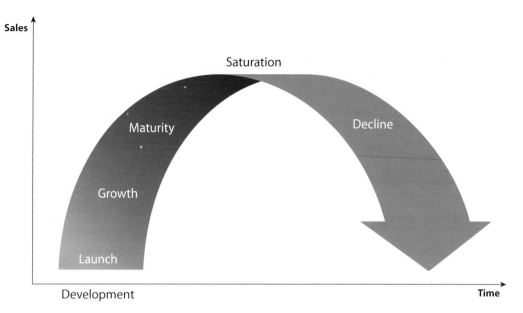

The product life cycle

Stage	Description
1 Launch	The product is first brought out and introduced to the shops.
2 Growth	Sales grow as the product is advertised and becomes well known.
3 Maturity	Sales slow down. Most people have one, and now there are competing products.
4 Saturation	Sales start to go down. Everybody's got one already. There are many competing products, which are often cheaper and better.
5 Decline	Sales fall further. The product is eventually withdrawn from the market.

- The normal product life cycle is shown here. Each stage can be a short or long time. This will differ from product to product. The stages in the life cycle are:
  - development — during which no sales are made, but there are costs
  - launch — when the product is first offered for sale; costs can be high as the product needs to be advertised
  - growth — as sales grow, competitors will begin to think about bringing out rival products
  - maturity — many people have bought the product but there are now also competitors; promotion is still needed
  - decline — sales fall and the business must decide whether to try to extend the life cycle or let the product die
- Successful products can have their life cycle extended through product **extension strategies**. These may be changes to the product; finding new uses or applications; or additional promotion. These could add costs to the business but should also increase sales.

> **Speak the language**
>
> **product portfolio** — the range of products offered by a business
>
> **product life cycle** — the way in which a product is born, grows and dies
>
> **extension strategy** — a way to make the life cycle longer

In a nutshell

* Growing businesses can broaden their product portfolio.
* This helps them to compete.
* All products pass through a life cycle.
* Businesses use different ways to support the product at different stages.
* At launch, techniques to encourage product trial are used.
* Product extension strategies can be used to extend product life.

Boost your grade   **AO3:** do not forget the importance of branding when a business creates a product range. Mentioning the term 'branding' as a way to 'differentiate' products clearly puts you at AO3 knowledge levels.

Test yourself

Try this exam-style question.

1 Describe 'launch' and the two stages that follow it in a product life cycle.   *(3 marks)*

2 Explain why a particular marketing technique might be used in the first of these stages.   *(3 marks)*

Managing a brand: the Boston matrix

What the specification requires

You need to know how a business builds its brands both to keep existing customers and to attract new customers (repeat purchase and product trial). You need to understand how a business uses brands to make its products stand out from competitors. You should be able to use the Boston matrix to analyse a product portfolio.

In brief

The **product portfolio** refers to the various products a business offers for sale. As a business grows, it can increase its portfolio to create a wider range. A wider and more balanced range helps it to compete. Brands are used and developed to support **product trial** and **repeat purchases**. This is one way to differentiate products from the competition. The Boston matrix is a tool that can be used to analyse which brands are succeeding and which should be dropped.

Revision notes

- Product portfolios can be analysed and managed using the Boston matrix to examine the position of each of a business's products in its product portfolio.
- The matrix plots how important each product is in its own market by showing market share for the product against the potential for growth in that market.
- Products are put into one of four categories called 'stars', 'problem children', 'cash cows' and 'dogs'.
- Stars have a high market share in a fast-growing market — they may have been first into a new market (called a 'blue-sky' market). They need high marketing expenditure to keep them competitive.

The Boston matrix

- Problem children may also be known as 'question marks' — these products have a small market share in a fast-growing market and could provide high future profits.
- Cash cows have a large market share in a mature or slow-growing market. These are established brands that need little marketing expenditure. Often these are market leaders that produce cash to support other products. Bassett's jelly babies and Nestlé's Polo mints are examples.
- Dogs are products with a small share of a slow-growing market — they probably cost more than they are worth to maintain.
- Marketing managers choose whether to keep or lose each product (hold or divest). The most usual tactics will be to:
  - keep the cows, using the cash to support other products (milking the cows)
  - hold the stars; try to turn them into cash cows by using profits from existing cows
  - build the problem children; try to turn them into stars by using profits from the cash cows
  - divest the dogs; try to get rid of poorly performing products, preferably by selling them off

Speak the language

product portfolio — the various products that a business offers for sale

product trial — when a customer buys a product for the first time, 'just to try it'

repeat purchase — when a customer has a good first experience with a product, so returns to buy more

In a nutshell

∗ Businesses develop their product portfolios to attract a wider range of customers.
∗ They have to try new products so that customers can trial them.
∗ If they have established products, they can use these to support the launch and growth of new products.
∗ The Boston matrix is a useful tool to see how well products are performing.

Boost your grade **AO2 to AO3:** you should be able not only to explain how the Boston matrix works and why it is useful, but also to link this to how the marketing mix could change as a result of the analysis. Use current examples of brands to support explanations.

Test yourself

1 Draw a Boston matrix (without looking at the diagram on page 82).

2 Give one reason why it is a valuable tool for a business.

Topic 26
Building a successful marketing mix: price

What the specification requires

Price is just one part of the marketing mix, but it can be used to support business growth. Various pricing strategies can be used to gain market share and to compete more effectively. You should understand the factors that influence such pricing decisions.

In brief

Businesses can use effective **pricing techniques** to increase market share, to compete effectively and to further their growth. You should understand how such pricing decisions may be used, and how they are more or less effective according to the type of market in which the business operates and the degree of competition that it faces. You should also remember that businesses have to set prices so that they are competing and attracting customers. Some businesses are able to take a loss on certain products for a period, and this makes them more effective competitors in a market.

Fotolia

A £5,000 wedding dress: how much is cost, how much is mark-up?

Revision notes

- The most common form of pricing is **cost-plus pricing**. This is where the business adds up the various costs of producing the product and then adds on a percentage for profit (called a **mark-up**).
- Most other methods of pricing are competitive, as they involve pricing in such a way that the business's products sell more than its competitors' products. Smaller businesses may not have access to these methods, whereas growing businesses will. Typical pricing strategies include:
  - skimming — where a product (often new technology) can be sold at an opening high price to those who want to be first to own it
  - penetration pricing — where a product can be sold at an opening low price to gain market share
  - loss leaders — where a product is priced so low that it does not even cover its costs. This attracts buyers who

realise the benefits of the product and continue to buy it. In retail terms it is usually a staple product (such as bread or milk), priced to attract customers into the shop so that they spend money on other products

- Pricing strategies such as these can only be used where a business has a dominant position in a market, such as having a new product, or where competitors cannot afford to match prices.

- Some competitive pricing involves looking at what rivals are charging and matching this price. Businesses with a larger share of the market will be able to control this price, whereas smaller businesses must just accept the 'normal' price for a product, as set by the market.

In a nutshell

* Most businesses will price to cover costs.
* Growing businesses may have access to other pricing strategies, and therefore may be able to compete more effectively.
* Some of these are used to gain a market position.
* Others are used to compete more effectively.
* Many small businesses do not have this power, and must accept the market price.

Boost your grade   **AO1 to AO2:** pricing techniques that you suggest must be suitable for both the product or brand and the market in which the business is operating. A bakery, for example, would be unlikely to find skimming useful, as this is usually linked to new technology products.

Test yourself

Match the term on the left with the correct definition on the right.

1	cost-plus pricing	setting price to cover the costs of a product
2	loss leaders	the percentage added to the cost-plus price for profit
3	mark-up	an opening low price to gain market share
4	penetration pricing	an opening high price for a new product
5	skimming	a price so low that it does not even cover its costs

Topic 27

Building a successful marketing mix: promotion

What the specification requires

You should know that promotional activities can be used to help and support brands as just one part of the marketing mix. Larger businesses can choose from a range of appropriate promotional methods. Businesses need to choose promotions carefully, taking into account the product itself, the market in which they are operating and the likely reaction of competitors.

In brief

Larger businesses may have more effective **promotional strategies**, first because they can afford them and second because, as they grow larger, they need to use them to reach wider markets. Methods that are not suitable for smaller businesses, such as television or national billboard campaigns, are more expensive but may also be more effective. Any method that is used will only be effective if it is appropriate to the product and effective in the market. The use of promotion in a competitive market may be countered by other businesses increasing their own levels of promotion.

Revision notes

- Growing businesses are able to afford a much wider range of promotional strategies than small businesses.
- Advertising is publicity for a product that is paid for directly; it is called **above-the-line** expenditure. Advertising is used to promote products through broadcast and print media, such as television, radio, posters, magazines, leaflets and point-of-sale material. Larger businesses can afford to use outlets such as television. Such outlets tend to be more effective as they reach a wider audience. However, they are also more expensive.
- Sales promotion is called **below-the-line** expenditure. Growing businesses can

Larger businesses can afford to sponsor events such as Formula 1 racing

use sales promotion techniques such as loss leaders (see page 84), special offers (such as 'buy one, get one free'), competitions, money-off coupons, free samples and trials, joint promotions with other businesses (e.g. washing powders recommended by washing-machine manufacturers) and loyalty cards. Growing businesses may also be able to market and sell directly to the customer, through websites or catalogues, for example. This is called direct marketing.

- Sponsorship means that the product will be associated with a certain event or sport, or what is good about the event — a marathon race could promote fitness, for instance. Larger businesses can afford to sponsor larger and more recognised teams, events or organisations.
- The business should choose the promotional mix that is going to be most effective in its target market. This depends on the nature of the market (e.g. is it a market leader; does it have power in the market?), the type of product (e.g. is it essential or easily substituted?), and how competitors react to increased promotion.

In a nutshell

* Bigger businesses can use a wider range of promotional strategies.
* They can afford sales promotions.
* They can use national advertising media.
* They can sponsor big, well-recognised events.

Speak the language

promotional strategies — any method designed to increase awareness and sales of a product

above-the-line — directly paid-for advertising

below-the-line — promotions that increase sales, but are not advertising

Boost your grade

AO3: you should be able to argue for and against promotion and then form a judgement. The main case for it is that it informs — without it customers would not know what was on offer and would therefore not be able to make a choice. The case against it is that it is an unnecessary cost, which is passed on to the consumer.

Test yourself

Fill in the missing words from the list below. If you are feeling confident, cover the words and do the exercise from memory.

A business should choose the .... that is going to be most effective in its

.... This depends on the nature of the ...., the type of ....

and how .... react to increased promotion. Larger businesses can afford better

..........................., such as .... like competitions and .... with other

businesses. They can also sell directly to customers through .... They can afford

.... of well-known teams or events.

competitors   joint promotions   market   product   promotional mix

promotional techniques   sales promotions   sponsorship   target market   websites

Topic 28
Building a successful marketing mix: place

What the specification requires

You should understand that, as a business succeeds, it may need to access a wider customer base. To do so may mean that it needs to broaden the distribution channels it already has, or add new channels to reach more potential customers. You should be able to match appropriate sales outlet and distribution channels, and recognise that this is just one part of the marketing mix.

In brief

A growing business will need to access more customers, so may need more, or better, distribution channels. Most businesses sell to wholesalers or retailers, but could also extend their reach by selling directly to customers. This could be via direct sales, telephone sales or the internet. Using the internet as a channel of distribution for direct sales is the most popular and successful route for many businesses. The choice of distribution channel will be affected by the nature of the product, the customers and the market in which the business operates.

Revision notes

- **Place** refers to where a product is sold and how the product gets there. Growing businesses may need to choose different locations to sell and **channels of distribution** to access a larger customer base. The main channels used by businesses are:
  - Retail outlets, ranging from small corner shops to hypermarkets and department stores. Many outlets still specialise in a particular product, while others offer a general range. Some major retailers will not offer shelf space to more than the brand leader and their own brand. This can be a problem for products that are popular but not leaders.
  - Wholesalers. These allow the business to sell bulk stock, making room for new production. However, wholesalers will not pay as high a price for products as either retailers or consumers.

> **Speak the language**
>
> **place** — both sales location and how goods arrive there
>
> **channels of distribution** — ways to deliver goods to customers, or to where customers can buy them
>
> **cold calls** — sales telephone calls made when there has been no previous contact with the customer

- Telesales. This is are where products are sold directly to consumers via a telephone call. Often telesales is done to sell additional products to those already owned (e.g. additional insurance or a new banking service). **Cold calls** do not tend to be very effective.
- Mail-order. Here a business provides a catalogue or advertises in a newspaper or magazine. Such direct sales are only possible where delivery costs are not a major factor.

■ With internet sales, products are delivered to buyers. The product range can be viewed via a website. Websites open up worldwide markets but, again, delivery costs may be a major factor.

■ To judge whether or not a distribution channel is appropriate, a business needs to consider its own needs and those of its customers. Important factors for the business are cost, availability and profit margins. Important factors for customers are convenience, cost and reliability.

Internet sales have opened up markets worldwide

In a nutshell

✳ Growing businesses may need to access more customers.
✳ To do this, they may need more distribution channels.
✳ This could mean using more traditional channels, such as retailers.
✳ It may mean using more modern channels, such as the internet.

Test yourself

Try this exam-style question.

Aroma Plus is a company that sells a range of natural products. It has a website that tells visitors the location of the nearest outlet and provides details of the range of goods on offer. Customers can buy a limited range of goods from the site.

Discuss whether Aroma Plus should increase the range of goods it sells on its website. *(6 marks)*

AO2 to AO3: you should try to show the depth of your understanding by using recent examples. For example, many questions on distribution will be talking about online sales and how these have changed the market. You will gain AO3 marks by using this in your reasoning.

Section test: Marketing

1 Which of the following is NOT a main source for desk research?
   (a) books
   (b) newspapers and journals
   (c) questionnaires
   (d) internet

2 Which of the following is NOT a feature of field research?
   (a) It is targeted.
   (b) It is up to date.
   (c) It is inexpensive.
   (d) It is time-consuming.

3 The Boston matrix can be used by a business to see
   (a) how a market is changing
   (b) how a product is performing
   (c) how the product life cycle is developing
   (d) what a competitor is doing

4 A narrow product mix means that
   (a) the business makes products and services
   (b) the business makes a range of goods
   (c) the business concentrates on a few products
   (d) the business sells a range of services

5 Creating a memorable name or image for a product is called
   (a) product recognition
   (b) targeted advertising
   (c) product mixing
   (d) branding

6 Where a product fails to live up to expectations, its life cycle is said to be
   (a) shortened
   (b) extended
   (c) aborted
   (d) saturated

7 Which of the following is NOT a recognised part of a product life cycle?
   (a) development
   (b) maturity
   (c) decline
   (d) popularity

8 Cost-plus pricing is calculated as
   (a) fixed cost plus variable cost
   (b) cost plus mark-up
   (c) start-up cost plus variable cost
   (d) revenue minus costs

9 Below-the-line promotion is
   (a) paid-for advertising
   (b) not-paid-for advertising
   (c) not directly paid-for advertising
   (d) not very effective advertising

10 The traditional channel of distribution involving manufacturers, wholesalers and retailers is called
   (a) short chain
   (b) long chain
   (c) complex distribution
   (d) intermediate distribution

Topic 29
Research and good design

What the specification requires

You need to know that one way in which a business can make its products stand out from others is through good design. This is a form of **product differentiation**, like branding. Businesses have a better chance of success if their products have unique features or properties.

In brief

Customers may demand a product for a number of different reasons. They may want it because it is within their price range, because it is fashionable or desirable, or because it does the job it is supposed to do. A coat may have a **function** (to keep you warm and dry), be fashionable (perhaps have a designer label) and be at the right price.

Revision notes

- Product designers have to balance several elements when making new products. They look at how the product will do its job (function), how it will look (known as its **aesthetic**) and how it can be sold at a competitive price.
- Sometimes one aspect wins out over another. A consumer may buy a coat because of its fashion label, rather than its primary function of keeping him or her warm.
- Research and development (R&D) will take place based on the design mix of function, aesthetic and cost. Sometimes it is hard to strike a good balance between all these. For example, cutting costs by using cheaper inputs or materials could affect function; improving appearance could increase costs, and so force a price increase.

How a product looks is often as important as its function

- For some businesses, function is most important — a new drug must work as it is supposed to, rather than look good. In other businesses, such as the fashion industry, function may take second place to how something looks — shoes may look fantastic, but be near-impossible to walk in!
- Remember, a quality product is one that does what it was designed to do. For example, a cheap umbrella is still a quality product as long as it keeps the rain off. An umbrella that leaks is not a quality product, however expensive it was!
- R&D departments (or businesses) try to develop products that have the balance that will attract the customer to buy. Scientific research is vital to making improvements.

In a nutshell

* Businesses try to make products stand out from the competition.
* This is called differentiation.
* Product designers need to balance elements when designing products.
* The product must fulfil its function, i.e. do its job.
* It can then be made to look good, providing this does not increase costs too much.
* R&D departments work to perfect this balance.

Test yourself

State whether each of the following statements is true or false.

1 A consumer will never buy a product that does not fulfil its function.

2 An expensive umbrella that leaks is a quality product because of its price.

3 Cutting costs by using cheaper inputs or materials will not affect function.

4 How the product will do its job is referred to as its 'function'.

5 Improving the appearance of a product could increase costs.

6 In the fashion industry, the aesthetic may be more important than the product function.

7 Products can be over-priced if they fulfil their function and have a high aesthetic value.

8 'R&D' stands for 'research and development'.

9 A quality product is one that does not do what it was designed to do.

10 What a product looks like is known as its 'aesthetic'.

Boost your grade

AO2 to AO3: to reach AO3 marks you have to show that you can analyse a problem and then come to a decision — giving evidence to support why you have made that decision. For example, you may be asked both to describe the features of a product and to judge which of those features is most attractive to the average buyer.

Managing stock

What the specification requires

You should know what is meant by 'stock' in a business. You need to understand what is meant by stock control and how efficient stock control is linked to lower prices. You should be able to explain how a traditional stock reordering system works.

In brief

Businesses may have to hold a certain amount of stock, or **inventories**. This could be in the form of raw materials, partly finished goods, components, spares for machinery or even finished products. The amount held will depend on the type of business. If stock is highly valuable, or perishable, or expensive to store, the business may hold little of it. If it is hard to obtain or takes a long time to deliver, the business may be forced to hold high levels. There is a cost attached to holding any stock, so managing the quantity held is important in order to keep costs down.

Revision notes

- Businesses need systems to keep track of stock in order to ensure that they have the right amount of stock for their immediate needs. Stock includes everything the business might need for production, from raw materials through components and part-finished product to stocks of the final product.
- Stock is usually referred to, and shown in accounts, as 'inventories'.
- Holding stock costs money, so it is important for a business to hold as little as possible, but sufficient for its needs. It must strike a balance between holding too much stock and holding too little. Holding too much stock means costs that could be avoided. Not holding enough could mean loss of production or sales.
- Traditional stock graphs look like the graph shown here. A maximum and minimum stock level is established. Once

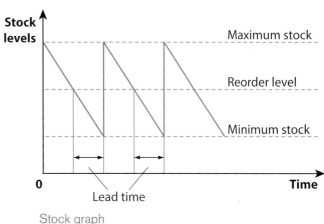

Stock graph

stock falls below a certain level (the reorder level), more is ordered. This new stock takes time to arrive (called **lead time**) and is, ideally, delivered as stock reaches its minimum level. As an insurance, many businesses hold more than this level of stock so that there is a buffer against a shortfall or a delay. This is called **buffer stock**.

■ **Just-in-time** (JIT) stock control plans for stock to arrive just as it is needed, as opposed to holding stock **just-in-case.** Just-in-time is cheaper and more efficient than just-in-case, but carries risks if stock fails to arrive.

In a nutshell

* All businesses need inventories of some sort, such as materials, components and finished stock.
* All stock that is held costs the business money.
* Stock systems attempt to anticipate when new stock will be needed.
* Some systems hold stock against possible delays.
* Just-in-time systems try to make sure stock arrives exactly as it is needed

Test yourself

Complete and label the stock flow diagram below (without looking at page 93).

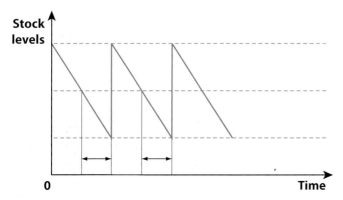

Topic 31
Managing quality

What the specification requires

You need to understand that quality is important to a business, to keep customers happy. Businesses therefore try to ensure quality output either by checking quality at each stage or at the end of production, or by having a culture of quality throughout the business.

In brief

To a business, **quality** is about producing goods or carrying out services with as few flaws or problems as possible. All production that is not up to quality standards is wasted, and therefore adds to costs. To a customer, a quality good or service is one that does what it is supposed to do. It is one that is, in UK law, 'fit for purpose'. If the product or service does not do as promised, then the consumer has the right to demand his or her money back. It is therefore vital to businesses to ensure that they are checking quality.

Revision notes

- It is important for a business to maintain quality. This can be achieved through **quality control** (i.e. checking quality at the end of production) or **quality assurance**, where it becomes everyone's responsibility to maintain quality at every stage of production.
- Traditional quality control systems check that the finished product has reached the required standard. The problem with this system is that the product has already been made, and must therefore be wasted if it is not up to scratch. This is particularly true where a process is involved (e.g. baking and food manufacture, refining and painting). In these cases ingredients or other inputs cannot be recovered.
- **Total quality management** (TQM) is a system that was first developed in Japan. Everyone involved in production is responsible for quality. Each worker

Checking quality can be costly, but it is important for a firm's reputation

(and each machine) checks for quality as the product enters an area, as it is processed, and before it leaves. The 'total' also extends to parts, materials and other inputs. A truly TQM business will only deal with other TQM businesses.

- 'Kaizen' is another Japanese system. Here even the tiniest improvement is seen as making for better efficiency and quality. The term now means 'continuous improvement'.
- A business will usually set up its own quality systems to make sure that production standards are even better than the consumer expects. Businesses look at what the law requires and then add to this to please the consumer and to beat competition.
- Managers keep a constant watch on costs to ensure that production is cost-effective. This means keeping costs down to allow prices to remain competitive. However, costs should not be cut at the expense of quality.
- Businesses can earn international quality standards such as ISO 9001.

In a nutshell

* Businesses will be concerned with the quality of their production.
* They will want to keep costs down by having as few faults as possible.
* They can check quality at each stage of production. This is inefficient and causes waste.
* They can make it everyone's responsibility to check. This is called TQM and extends even to the suppliers of the business.

Speak the language

quality — describes a good or service that does what it is supposed to do

quality control — systems that check that the finished product has reached the required standard

quality assurance — where quality systems are built into a process

total quality management (TQM) — all workers are responsible for quality at all stages

Test yourself

Match the correct term on the left with its description on the right.

1	cost-effective production	production with as few faults as possible
2	ISO 9001	a system to ensure quality through continuous improvement
3	kaizen	an international standard of quality
4	quality (to a business)	a product that does the job it is supposed to do
5	quality (to a consumer)	a system to check that finished goods are perfect
6	quality assurance	keeping costs down so that the business is competitive
7	quality control	a system where every person and business involved in production ensures quality
8	TQM	a system that checks quality at all stages of the production process

Boost your grade

AO1: accurate use of terms will bring you AO1 knowledge marks. Don't confuse 'quality' with 'expensive' or 'cheap'. Quality has nothing to do with the price of a good or service. A quality product is just one that does as it should. A match that strikes first time is as much a quality product as a diamond engagement ring.

Topic 32
Customer service

What the specification requires

You need to understand that businesses have to keep **customers** happy in order to keep them returning. You should know that they do this by providing good levels of customer service. You should understand why it is important to a business to have loyal customers, who bring repeat trade.

In brief

Businesses need to encourage **customer loyalty** by providing good levels of service. Businesses need to know information about their customers, including how satisfied they are with the service that they are receiving. Customer service is used to attract customers and, more importantly, to keep them. It is much cheaper for a business to retain customers than it is for the business to try and win new ones.

Revision notes

- Businesses need to provide customers with the appropriate level of service. This is linked to what the customer expects. The right level of service matches customer expectations. Customers who are happy will return. It is much more efficient to keep the customers that the business already has than to attract new ones.
- The business should learn what its customers want in terms of service, and provide it. This could include speed of response, range of goods, prices, ease of payment, deliveries, etc. Specific wants will be linked to specific businesses. Businesses will lose customers if they do not provide good levels of service. The four most common parts to customer service are:
  - providing information
  - giving advice
  - after-sales service
  - providing convenient ways to pay

Giving information on packaging is an important part of customer service

- There is a difference between the customer and the **consumer**. The customer is the person who actually buys the product. They may be buying it for their own use, in which case they are also the consumer. Alternatively, they may be buying it for someone else, such as a child, a partner or a friend, and for other reasons than their own wants or needs. Businesses recognise this and tend to aim marketing at the consumer.

Speak the language

customer loyalty — repeat business from customers who return

customer — the person or business that buys the product

consumer — the person, business or organisation that is the final user of the product

- The distinction is important, as the customer is the one who has to be happy at the point of purchase. He or she has to find the retail outlet convenient and expects good service and advice. The consumer expects the products bought to be of good quality and to do what they are supposed to do. This is covered by consumer protection.

In a nutshell

* Businesses should provide the service levels that customers expect.
* If they do, this will bring repeat business.
* There are four main aspects to customer service.
* Customers expect accurate information, advice, after-sales service and convenient ways to pay.
* Satisfied customers become repeat customers; this is vital for business survival.

Boost your grade

AO1 to AO2: different aspects of customer service will have different emphases depending on the type of business. This is why you should always read the mini-case-study carefully.

Test yourself

Draw up a table with the four aspects of customer service as headings and list the terms below under the appropriate heading.

Providing information	Giving advice	After-sales service	Providing convenient ways to pay

accurate   as required   cards   cash   clear   credit

delivery   helpful   packaging   specialist   warranties

Topic 33
Consumer protection

What the specification requires

Some businesses may try to cheat customers, but there are consumer protection laws to counter this. These laws influence the way businesses operate. You may be asked to explain the basic principles of protection provided by the Trade Descriptions Act and the Sale of Goods Act.

In brief

The government has passed laws to protect consumers against businesses that might try to cheat them, or rob them of value. Products bought should be as described, fit for purpose and not faulty or dangerous. Businesses have to make sure that what they are offering for sale is not in breach of any of the legislation. Businesses should treat fairly with consumers; this includes being clear about charges and penalties, and using accurate weights and measures.

Revision notes

- Customers expect a quality good or service. This means one that is fit for purpose (i.e. does what it is supposed to do).
- Businesses should deal fairly with customers. In the UK the first line of defence is the customer. Customers should make sure that they have bought the right product for the purpose and have read, understood and followed any instructions that come with it. The Latin tag for this is **caveat emptor**, which means 'let the buyer beware'.
- There are laws to protect the consumer. For example, the Trade Descriptions Act makes sure that labels and other information is accurate and that descriptions of products are accurate (even in advertisements).

Customers should find six large, free-range eggs inside this box

- The Sale of Goods Act and the Supply of Services Act say that goods must be of a satisfactory quality to be sold and should meet the purpose for which they are sold. These Acts guarantee when customers are entitled to replacements or refunds. They also give the customer, in the case of a service not being properly carried out, the right to have a refund or a replacement service charged to the original business.

- Inspectors are employed by local government to check hygiene in places preparing, serving or selling food, and to check the accuracy of weights and measures being used.
- Some consumer protection exists outside the law, such as through industry bodies and the British Standards Institute, which tests products and awards the BSI **Kitemark** to those that meet its standards.

In a nutshell

* Customers have a duty to make sure they are buying the right product for the purpose.
* Some laws protect consumers.
* The main ones are the Trade Descriptions Act and the Sale of Goods Act.
* They ensure that customers receive fair treatment.
* Some consumer protection exists outside the law.

Test yourself

Choose the most appropriate answer from each of the choices below.

1 All products bought should be quality products, i.e. they should be **(a)** expensive, **(b)** exclusive, **(c)** fit for purpose, **(d)** delivered.

2 The Sale of Goods Act and the Supply of Services Act **(a)** inspect all products before they are sold, **(b)** guarantee when consumers are entitled to replacements or refunds, **(c)** guarantee that all goods are value for money, **(d)** check all weights and measures to make sure that they are accurate.

3 'Caveat emptor' is the Latin tag that means **(a)** 'let the buyer beware', **(b)** 'let the seller be careful', **(c)** 'the price is right', **(d)** 'the cave is empty'.

4 The Kitemark is the mark of quality applied by **(a)** the Basic Standards Institute, **(b)** the British Standards Institute, **(c)** the British Sanitary Institute, **(d)** the Basic Standards Institution.

5 Local government inspectors **(a)** inspect all products before they are sold, **(b)** guarantee when consumers are entitled to replacements or refunds, **(c)** guarantee that all goods are value for money, **(d)** check all weights and measures to make sure that they are accurate.

Boost your grade

AO1: you will almost never be asked for a specific date or law. To gain knowledge marks you do not need to remember laws, but should be able to talk about what consumer law is basically for, and some of its main features.

Section test: Meeting customer needs

1 Which of the following is not one of the main parts of customer service?
   (a) providing information
   (b) giving advice
   (c) after-sales service
   (d) packing customers' bags

2 The missing major aspect of customer service in question 1 is
   (a) delivery
   (b) putting up a website
   (c) providing convenient ways to pay
   (d) being polite

3 The most important requirement of customer information on a product is that it is
   (a) prominent
   (b) accurate
   (c) detailed
   (d) printed

4 All products bought should be quality products, i.e. they should be:
   (a) expensive
   (b) exclusive
   (c) fit for purpose
   (d) delivered

5 The Trade Descriptions Act says that
   (a) descriptions of products must be accurate, except in advertisements
   (b) you can have a 'cooling off' period after buying something
   (c) descriptions of products in advertisements must be accurate
   (d) it is up to the customer to decide whether descriptions of products are accurate

6 Which of the following is true? Using a total quality management system
   (a) means that finished production is checked for total quality
   (b) means that even suppliers should be part of the system
   (c) means that there will always be continuous improvement
   (d) is not appropriate for businesses that use processes, such as baking

7 'Caveat emptor' is the Latin tag that means
   (a) the price is right
   (b) the cave is empty
   (c) let the seller be careful
   (d) let the buyer beware

8 The most important feature in a new drug reaching the market would be
   (a) function
   (b) price
   (c) aesthetic
   (d) cost

9 Just-in-time stock control systems achieve all of the following EXCEPT one. Choose the odd one out.
   (a) It plans for stock to arrive just as it is needed.
   (b) It is cheaper and more efficient than just-in-case
   (c) It makes sure stocks are always there on time.
   (d) It carries risks to the business if stock fails to arrive.

10 The Kitemark is the mark of quality applied by
   (a) the Basic Standards Institute
   (b) the British Sanitation Institute
   (c) the British Standards Institute
   (d) the Basic Standards Institution

Topic 34
Managing cash flow

What the specification requires

You need to understand that cash flows into and out of a business, and these flows need to be managed. You may need to be able to forecast from cash-flow statements and should understand what cash-flow problems might arise and how the business might solve them.

In brief

A business has a constant flow of cash in and out. Cash comes in through sales revenue and flows out to pay for costs. A business needs enough cash to meet its day-to-day needs. The problem with cash is that the flows of it into and out of a business are never equal, so the business needs to manage these **cash flows**. You need to identify which cash flows are really under the control of managers.

Revision notes

- Cash comes into a business from sales and other income. Cash leaves the business as a result of costs and expenses. A **cash-flow forecast** is a planning tool that helps the business to see if it will have too much, or too little, cash for its needs. If there is more cash coming in than the business needs, this is called a cash surplus. If there is less cash than it needs, this is called a cash shortage.
- A cash surplus costs the business, as the cash could be earning money if it was invested. A cash shortage costs the business because it will have to borrow to cover the shortfall.

ICT software can be used to forecast flows of cash

- Cash-flow forecasts help the business to avoid problems. Techniques to even out cash flows include spreading payments (e.g. making monthly payments rather than facing an annual bill), rescheduling payments (paying a bill later or arranging better credit terms with, for example, suppliers) and arranging to receive revenue sooner or more regularly (e.g. getting customers to pay in instalments).
- Businesses may also decide not to add to stock, but run down the stock they have. This increases inflows and decreases outflows.
- One of the major reasons for businesses to fail is cash shortages (a **cash-flow crisis**). Even if a business has full order books and is in profit, it cannot survive if it is unable pay its immediate bills.

In a nutshell

* Cash flows into and out of a business.
* These flows need to be managed.
* Too much cash is a waste of resources.
* Too little cash could lead to business failure.
* Businesses develop techniques to even out cash flows.

Speak the language

cash flow — money flowing into and out of a business

cash-flow forecast — a prediction of future flows

cash-flow crisis — when there is insufficient cash to pay immediate bills

Boost your grade

AO2 to AO3: for AO3 marks you should be able to explain which costs and revenue are really under the control of managers in a given situation, and which are outside their control. You can then recommend what action could be taken to improve cash flow.

Test yourself

Try this exam-style question.

Below are the predicted cash-flow figures for a business for the next 6 months.

	Cash in	Cash out
Opening balance	1,000	
January	1,000	7,000
February	7,000	4,000
March	1,000	500
April	500	0
May	2,000	500
June	1,500	500

(a) Draw up a cash-flow forecast using the figures given. *(6 marks)*

(b) What recommendation would you make to this business? *(6 marks)*

Topic 35
Improving profitability

What the specification requires

You need to know the difference between cash and profit, and how a business might try to improve its profitability. You need to recognise that improving profit is not always easy, and some actions will bring problems that outweigh any benefits.

In brief

Businesses try to break even (to make sure that costs are covered by **revenues**) and then to make a **profit**. Levels of profit — or profitability — can be increased by making **factors of production** work more efficiently. Managers can also try to increase profits by cutting costs or increasing revenues. However, any action taken by a manager must be judged on its overall effect on the business, as there could be disadvantages to some actions.

Revision notes

- Managers can try to increase the profitability of a business by making it more efficient. This could mean more productive labour (in which case, providing good motivation could work) or more productive processes or machinery (which could mean new machines or better use of existing ones). Managers must be careful that any additional costs are covered by increased revenues.
- Profits can be increased by either cutting costs, increasing revenue, or both. In trying to do either, a business might bring about other consequences. For instance, cutting costs by cutting staff could leave remaining workers overworked and demotivated, and therefore less efficient. Cutting costs by cutting levels of stock might reduce storage and delivery charges, but leave the business with insufficient stock to be able to meet customer needs.

Depending on customers' reaction, lower prices can either increase or decrease both revenue and profit

- Managers can also try to increase revenue by increasing prices. Increasing price will only increase revenue if sales either stay the same or do not fall by much. If the increase in price leads to a large fall in sales, the business may actually suffer a fall in revenue. Sometimes a decrease in price will increase revenue, providing customers buy more as a result of the decrease.
- Businesses need to judge what will happen by knowing their market and estimating how their customers will react to a change in price.

Speak the language

revenue — the income of a business from sales

profit — the excess of revenue over costs

factors of production — inputs of land, labour and capital needed for production

In a nutshell

* Managers will try to improve the profitability of businesses.
* This can be achieved through more efficient use of inputs and resources.
* It can also be achieved through lower costs or higher revenues.
* Managers need to think through the possible consequences of changes that they are planning.

Test yourself

State whether each of the statements below is true or false.

1 Buying new machines will always improve efficiency.

2 Paying workers a higher wage will lead to improvements in efficiency and profitability.

3 One way to increase profit could be to decrease price, in order to increase sales and revenue.

4 Managers must be careful to make sure that additional costs are covered by increased revenues.

5 Greater efficiency can be gained through a better-motivated labour force.

6 Managers can try to increase the profitability of a business by making it more efficient.

7 The only way to increase profits is to cut costs.

8 Profits can be increased by cutting costs or increasing revenues.

9 Increases in price will always lead to increases in revenue.

10 If an increase in price leads to a large fall in sales, revenue could fall.

Boost your grade

AO2 to AO3: for AO3 marks you should be able to argue why a change may or may not work. For example, if you can explain why an increased price does not always bring about increased revenue, you will be working at AO3.

Breakeven analysis

What the specification requires

You will need to be able to identify the main types of cost faced by a business and to explain why they are important. You should understand how to calculate **breakeven** for a business and interpret it. You should know how breakeven analysis can be used as a tool by a business, and be able to use it yourself.

In brief

Businesses produce either a good or a service for sale. In either case there are costs. The money that the business receives for its sales is called **revenue**. Business costs are divided into **fixed costs**, also called indirect costs or overheads, and **variable costs**. Some costs are semi-variable, containing elements of both. Breakeven is where total costs equal total revenue. Changes in any cost, or in revenue from sales, will alter the breakeven point. Breakeven can be used as a tool to predict the effect of such changes.

Which item is contributing profit; which is making a loss?

Revision notes

- In the production of goods, or provision of services, there are costs.
- Costs may be fixed or variable. Total cost is fixed costs plus variable costs.
- Fixed costs do not vary with output. Examples are rent, interest payments and rates. They are paid whether or not a business is producing and regardless of how much a business is producing. Variable costs vary directly with output. Examples are raw materials, ingredients and power.
- Semi-variable costs vary with output, but not directly. For example, a business may need to pay overtime, or a shop to open for longer hours.
- Revenue is the money received from the sale of products or services.
- Breakeven is where total costs are equal to total revenue: where there is neither profit nor loss. Businesses may want

to ensure that they are not at, but above, breakeven, so that they are not in danger of making a loss. The amount by which they are above breakeven is called the margin of safety.

- Breakeven charts and graphs can be used to predict where a profit will be made, and can help the business to plan.
- To overcome the problems of inaccurate calculation using graphs, a formula can be used to work out the contribution of each sale towards breakeven. There are two parts to the formula:

contribution to fixed costs = price per unit – variable cost per unit

$$\text{breakeven level of sales} = \frac{\text{fixed costs}}{\text{contribution}}$$

- Breakeven is valuable to a business for 'what if?' scenarios, to predict what would happen if factors like costs, revenues and sales changed.

In a nutshell

- * Businesses produce goods or services for sale at a price and this involves costs.
- * Costs can be listed in many different ways.
- * When total cost equals total revenue, breakeven has been reached.
- * Any change in cost or revenue affects breakeven.
- * Breakeven can be used as a tool to predict 'what if?' scenarios.

Test yourself

Copy the graph below and insert the correct labels.

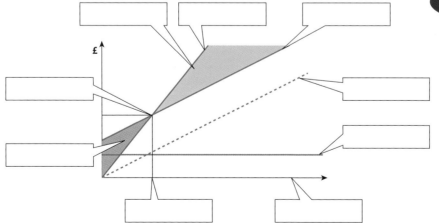

Boost your grade

AO2 to AO3: with the Applied qualification it is important that you not only work out breakeven from information you are given, but use it to suggest changes or improvements to the business.

Topic 37
Financing growth

What the specification requires

Larger businesses may need different sources of finance as they grow. You should be able to recognise the advantages and disadvantages of each method of internal and external finance in a given situation. Two key considerations for a business are the amount of risk involved and the amount of control that has to be given up or shared.

In brief

A larger business can access different sources of finance. The main methods may be split into internal and external sources. **Internal sources** include retained profits and the sale of unwanted assets. **External sources** include share issues — either becoming a public limited company or, as a plc, issuing more shares. Large businesses can also access larger loans, and are likely to have more **assets**, such as land and property, on which they can raise funds by using them as mortgage security.

Public limited companies can raise finance by selling shares via the Stock Exchange

Revision notes

- As a business grows, it may have more ways to raise finance than a smaller business. It is likely to have more assets, more profit and a better reputation than a small business, and this may help it to raise finance from different sources.
- Although **retained profit** is a source of finance for all businesses, a larger business may have more profit, and this is therefore a more realistic source of finance for larger businesses than for smaller ones. This is an important internal source. Because it is internal, interest does not have to be paid and the finance does not have to be repaid. The main disadvantage may be to shareholders, who do not receive as high a share of the profit.

- A further internal source is the sale of unwanted assets. If a business has an asset that it no longer needs or uses, it can sell it off. For example, selling redundant equipment might allow for the purchase of larger plant for increased production.
- Limited companies have access to finance through the sale of shares. A private limited company might decide to **float** on the stock market by inviting the public to buy shares, and thus become a public limited company (plc). Plcs can also raise additional finance by selling more shares. However, each share has a right to part of the profit and to a say in how the business operates. This can make running the business difficult.
- External sources include the usual range of secured loans (e.g. mortgages) and unsecured loans available to business: in other words, increases in debt.

Speak the language

internal sources of finance — finance that comes from within the business

external sources of finance — finance that comes from outside the business

asset — something that a business owns

retained profit — profit that is not distributed to owners

floating a company — offering shares in the company to the public, via the stock exchange

In a nutshell

* Large businesses have more sources of finance that they can access.
* Internal sources include retained profits and the sale of assets.
* External sources include the sale of shares.
* Other sources, such as banks, may be persuaded to make larger loans, as a large business may have more security.

Test yourself

Choose the most appropriate answer from each of the choices below.

1 A growing business is likely to have more of which of the following, to help it raise finance? **(a)** products, **(b)** people, **(c)** assets, **(d)** liabilities

2 Retained profit is what sort of finance? **(a)** internal, **(b)** external, **(c)** long-term, **(d)** short-term

3 Asset sales are what sort of finance? **(a)** internal, **(b)** external, **(c)** long-term, **(d)** short-term

4 Sales of shares on the stock market are what sort of finance? **(a)** internal, **(b)** external, **(c)** long term, **(d)** short term

5 Selling shares on the stock market is called **(a)** sinking a business, **(b)** floating a product, **(c)** sinking money into a company, **(d)** floating a company

AO1: AO1 marks may be linked to the accuracy of your use of terms. You should therefore make sure that you know the difference between internal and external sources of finance for a large business.

Section test: Effective financial management

1 Cash-flow forecasts are used to help planning. Techniques to even out cash flows include all of the following EXCEPT
   (a) making monthly payments rather than facing an annual bill
   (b) arranging better credit terms with suppliers
   (c) keeping any excess cash in a secure place on the premises
   (d) rescheduling payments so that they fall due at a later date
   (e) persuading customers to pay for products in advance

2 Managers can improve the profitability by all of the following EXCEPT
   (a) increasing prices so that revenue increases
   (b) lowering prices so that revenue increases
   (c) increasing the efficiency of the labour force
   (d) sacking some of the labour force so that the rest have to work harder
   (e) bringing in new or better machinery

3 Fixed costs are costs that
   (a) do not change
   (b) change with output
   (c) do not change with output
   (d) always stay the same
   (e) do not change very much

4 Revenue is defined as
   (a) price × number sold
   (b) price × fixed costs
   (c) price × variable costs
   (d) fixed costs × variable costs
   (e) fixed costs + variable costs

5 Which of the following is most likely to be an example of a variable cost?
   (a) rent
   (b) rates
   (c) interest payments
   (d) raw materials
   (e) wages

6 The breakeven sales point is the point at which
   (a) sales are made
   (b) revenue is made
   (c) a profit is made
   (d) a loss is made
   (e) neither profit nor loss is made

7   Which financial format would usually include a prediction of borrowing requirements?
    (a) breakeven chart
    (b) balance sheet
    (c) cash-flow forecast
    (d) profit-and-loss account
    (e) statement of account

8   Which one of the following would probably be a suitable source of finance for a growing business?
    (a) retained profit
    (b) bank loan
    (c) overdraft
    (d) owners' funds
    (e) trade credit

9   Which one of the following would be considered a fixed cost?
    (a) raw materials
    (b) fuel
    (c) power
    (d) interest on a loan
    (e) cost of phone calls

10 Which of the following statements is NOT true?
    (a) A 'what if?' scenario is used to look into the future and make predictions.
    (b) Breakeven graphs can be used to look at 'what if' scenarios.
    (c) The breakeven point is where total cost equals total revenue.
    (d) Any change in either costs or revenues will affect breakeven.
    (e) Variable costs are not as important to breakeven as fixed costs.

Topic 38

Organisational structures and management

What the specification requires

You need to understand that larger businesses need more complex organisational structures than smaller ones. You should know how to read an organisational chart, and what the various relationships within it mean in terms of management. You should understand what is meant by centralisation and decentralisation, and the benefits and drawbacks to each.

In brief

For any business to operate at all (or any organisation, for that matter), it needs to have some sort of structure. Businesses are therefore organised in a number of different ways. This usually depends on their size, on the management style of the owners, or on the type of business or type of market they are in. Decision-making could be done in the centre, or delegated to managers throughout the organisation. The business could be split into divisions, and there could be different levels of management within a hierarchy.

Revision notes

- **Organisational charts** can show how a business is structured. The most common type is the family tree chart, showing each family of workers under a manager or director. Large

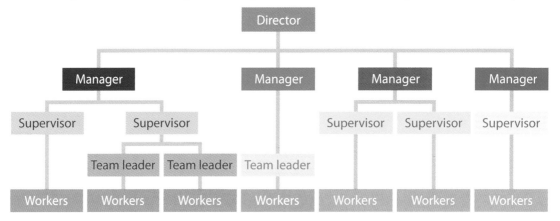

Family tree organisation chart

businesses are often split into divisions using this sort of structure. Divisions are usually based on product type, or location, or function (marketing, production, etc).

- Each manager has a number of people under his or her control. This is called the **span of control** and may be wide or narrow. The narrower the span, the more power the manager has over those underneath — his or her **subordinates**. This power, usually called **authority**, is the right within the organisational set-up to make decisions. In some cases, this authority may be passed on — this is called **delegation**.

- A **hierarchical structure** exists when each level of an organisation takes its direction from the level above, but has control over the levels below.
- Some organisations are controlled from the centre. This means that decisions are made by a few people. In an organisation that is very centrally controlled, there will be little delegation, and all decisions will be made at the top. This can mean quick decision-making. Sometimes the centre is too far away from the customer to be efficient.
- Decentralised organisations spread decision-making. This can mean better decisions made at local level.
- Some businesses have a vertical structure. This means that there are many layers but few people at each layer. Some businesses have a horizontal structure. This means there are few layers and many people at each layer.

Speak the language

organisational chart — diagram showing relationships in a business

span of control — the number of people for whom a manager is responsible

subordinates — those over whom someone else has power

authority — the power to take decisions

delegation — the right to pass on this power to others

hierarchical structure — where an organisation has levels of authority, with the smallest, and most powerful level, at the top

In a nutshell

* Businesses need to be organised.
* This is usually done in layers and, with larger businesses, into divisions.
* People higher up have authority over those lower down.
* Structures can affect decision-making and communication.

Boost your grade **AO2 to AO3:** you may be asked to analyse a business situation in order to make a decision. If you can link the levels of authority and motivation in a hierarchical structure to a theory — such as Maslow's (see Topic 39) — you will be operating at the top level.

Test yourself

Match the term on the left with the correct definition on the right.

1	authority	diagram showing relationships in a business
2	centralisation	the number of people for whom a manager is responsible
3	decentralisation	the right to pass on authority to others
4	delegation	decisions made by a few people
5	manager	decisions spread throughout the organisation
6	organisational chart	those over whom someone else has power
7	span of control	decision-making power
8	subordinates	a person with authority

Motivation

What the specification requires

You need to understand the importance of **motivation** in the workplace. You should be able to explain why a business prefers motivated workers. You should be able to analyse a business and apply a motivation theory, such as Maslow's, to its structure and staff. You should know how communication can affect motivation.

In brief

A worker who is motivated works because he or she wants to work. Businesses will therefore be keen to try and motivate workers. **Maslow's hierarchy of needs** is one way to look at motivation. Using this theory, managers can provide motivations for workers to reach the next level that they desire. Communication in an organisation can have an influence on motivation. For instance, where there are barriers to communication, motivation may be reduced.

Revision notes

- Maslow says workers work to satisfy certain needs. He says these needs are hierarchical — each level is reached from the level below. Once a level is achieved, the worker looks for the next level, until reaching the final goal. The levels of need are:
  1 Survival or subsistence — the basics, such as food and clothing. In a modern society, this means earning enough money to buy them.
  2 Security goals — wanting to feel safe and clear of threat.
  3 Social needs — people want to be part of a group or a family.
  4 Status — wanting to be respected and looked up to.
  5 **Self-actualisation** — the worker finally achieves their ultimate ambition.
- For a business, these needs might be seen as a decent wage, job security

Self-actualisation: a complicated way of saying you've got to where you want to be

Status: knowing that people look up to you

Social: having friends and family

Security: being able to plan for the future

Survival needs: food, water, shelter

Maslow's hierarchy of needs

and a pension, teamworking, a title or other symbol of status, and an achievement of some final goal — perhaps a certain job within the business.

- Not everyone agrees that these are what motivate people. Many say that workers are motivated from within, by a desire to do well, or to reach short-term goals such as a new car or a holiday.
- Communication up and down a hierarchy may be slow. Communication needs to be efficient. Lack of communication — or too much of it (instructions that are too detailed, for example) — will demotivate.

In a nutshell

* Workers are more efficient if they are motivated.
* Businesses are therefore keen to motivate workers.
* One theory says that workers are motivated by a set of needs.
* Others say that motivation comes from within.
* Poor organisation structure or communication can demotivate.

Test yourself

Copy the diagram below and fill in each level of Maslow's hierarchy of needs. Include an example at each level.

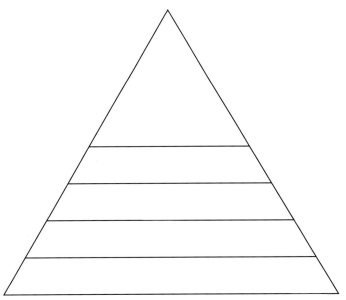

Topic 40
Remuneration

What the specification requires

You need to know about the various ways to pay staff, and how these can be used by a business to increase efficiency. You need to understand how different systems of payment will be viewed by both the employer and the employee.

In brief

It is vital to workers to know, first, that they will be paid for work done, and second, how they will be paid. This allows them to plan their expenditure and lifestyle with certainty. Different methods of payment reward different types of work and efficiency, and will therefore be used by different businesses according to their circumstances. To ensure flexibility, a business might use part-time staff rather than full-time employees. It will also make the choice between employing the specialists it needs all the time, or bringing outside expertise in when required.

Revision notes

- **Remuneration** refers to the way a worker is paid. Each type of payment system impacts on the business by having benefits and problems, as suggested below.
- Piece rates reward workers for the number of items made. This can encourage speed but this may be at the expense of quality or accuracy.
- Time rates are paid at an amount per period of time worked. The most common are weekly or monthly wages, or annual salaries. Workers who are paid a wage can normally earn **overtime** for extra time completed. Those on a salary have their annual amount divided by 12 months and receive this regardless of hours worked. Time rates can lead to workers working more slowly, but perhaps more accurately.
- Commission is a reward paid for increased sales. It is usually set as a percentage of all sales made above a base amount. This encourages salespeople to sell, but

One way to reward employees is through 'perks' such as company cars may lead to customer dissatisfaction if sales people put too much pressure on customers when trying to persuade them. It can also lead to low (or even no) pay for those salespeople who do not exceed the base target.

- Businesses need to employ a mixture of staff so that they have flexibility. They may employ full-time staff for positions where this is necessary and part-time staff to cover busy periods. They may also employ freelancers or other outside specialists to bring special skills to the business when needed.
- Other benefits may also form part of a remuneration package. These are often called 'perks'. These could include items such as pensions, company cars, canteens, staff discounts, **profit-sharing** and annual bonus payments.

In a nutshell

* Remuneration refers to the way workers are paid.
* Most payments are in money, but some are through 'perks'.
* Different systems are appropriate to different businesses.
* Each system has benefits and drawbacks.
* Businesses choose systems to give them efficiency and flexibility.

Boost your grade

AO2 to AO3: for AO3 marks you should be able to discuss the decisions that businesses have to make to keep wage costs down but remain flexible and efficient. For example, when would it be better to employ a freelance expert rather than have an expert employee on the books? You should also be able to consider the pros and cons of types of payment — does commission lead to pressure selling? Do piece rates lead to poor quality?

Test yourself

Match the terms on the left with the descriptions on the right.

1	commission	the way in which a worker is paid
2	freelancer	an amount paid per period of time worked
3	perks	an amount paid for the number of items made
4	piece rate	an amount paid for increased sales
5	remuneration	a person who offers his or her services to businesses on a temporary basis
6	time rate	benefits such as company cars, pension schemes and staff discounts

Section test: Effective people management

Bould's Garage Services Ltd is a private limited company owned by John Bould and his family. It is organised as shown in the chart below.

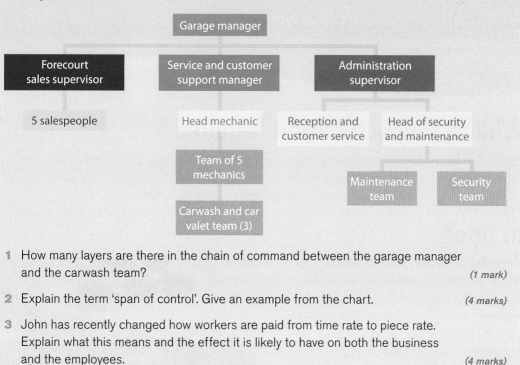

1 How many layers are there in the chain of command between the garage manager and the carwash team? *(1 mark)*

2 Explain the term 'span of control'. Give an example from the chart. *(4 marks)*

3 John has recently changed how workers are paid from time rate to piece rate. Explain what this means and the effect it is likely to have on both the business and the employees. *(4 marks)*

4 Recommend one way to motivate the staff using money and one way not using money. Explain your choices. *(6 marks)*

Total: 15 marks

Topic 41
Ethical issues affecting business

What the specification requires

You should understand the meaning of the term 'ethics' in business and why businesses are keen to be seen to be acting in an **ethical** manner. You should know that sometimes the ethical route is not the most profitable one, so this can cause conflict.

In brief

It is in the interests of businesses to have ethical policies. Such policies are often built into the aims and objectives of the business. Acting ethically means 'doing the right thing'. Examples include not testing products on animals, paying fair prices for materials and skills, not using cheap or child labour, and not carrying out production in dirty or dangerous conditions. Acting in an ethical way is often attractive to customers, so doing this helps to create customer loyalty.

Rainforest destruction allows for farms and trade — but at what cost?

Revision notes

- Businesses should act in ethical ways — that is, they should be moral in their actions. In practice, this means not harming the communities in which they produce and sell and not taking advantage of weak laws. They should also pay fair prices and not exploit producers or labour.
- Businesses are often keen to act ethically, as a good reputation in this area increases customer loyalty and sales.

- An ethical approach may have an impact on profits: for example, paying a fair price for supplies may mean paying a higher price. However, in the longer term, increased costs may be recovered through better sales as customers prefer to buy products that have been sourced and produced in an ethical manner.
- Many investors in businesses will only invest in those that have ethical policies. This is called **ethical investment**.
- **Pressure groups** are groups of people or organisations that try to influence businesses and governments to act in ethical ways (or what they consider to be ethical ways). Well-known pressure groups include the environmental group Greenpeace, the Worldwide Fund for Nature, PETA (People for the Ethical Treatment of Animals) and many charities. Pressure groups often use publicity gained from stunts to get their message across.
- Pressure groups may also reveal when businesses are acting unethically. They have challenged many major companies by finding child or cheap labour used in production, dangerous working conditions, or other unethical practices.

COOP

The Cooperative Group's investment in fair trade is an example of ethical trading

Speak the language

ethical — acting in a moral way

ethical investment — only investing in those businesses that have ethical standards

pressure groups — organisations that campaign for particular causes or changes

In a nutshell

* Businesses should act in a moral — or ethical — way.
* This might impact on profitability.
* An ethical approach is good for reputation and customer loyalty.
* An ethical approach may therefore be good for business.

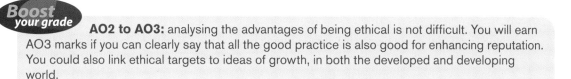

Boost your grade **AO2 to AO3:** analysing the advantages of being ethical is not difficult. You will earn AO3 marks if you can clearly say that all the good practice is also good for enhancing reputation. You could also link ethical targets to ideas of growth, in both the developed and developing world.

Test yourself

Read the following passage and answer the questions that follow as fully as possible.

Royaume Ltd is a worldwide business, specialising in sports equipment, sports clothing and sports shoes. Its head office is in Tinnerton, a new town about 15 miles from London, but it has operations all around the globe, including the European Union, North

and South America, and Asia, including the Far East. Royaume operates a 'fair trade' policy. It tries to buy locally sourced materials and makes sure that some of the profits from its operations are ploughed back into the countries where it works.

Some of the ethical credentials of Royaume were damaged last year by problems with an advertising campaign. Its Zipfast range of shoes had a graffiti-like logo which Muslim commentators pointed out spelt out an insult in Arabic. Also, the advertisement for the Zipfast range claimed that the product would help customers to run faster and recover from effort more quickly. These were claims that the business was unable to back up.

1 Explain what is meant by 'ethical constraints'. *(5 marks)*

2 Explain how Royaume may have breached these constraints and recommend what action the company should take. *(6 marks)*

3 Explain how the actions of the business might be seen as unethical. *(4 marks)*

Total: 15 marks

Topic 42
Environmental issues affecting business

What the specification requires

You should know how businesses can affect the environment: for example, through congestion and pollution. You should be aware of long-term environmental problems such as global warming. You should be aware of the sorts of policies that businesses use to be **environmentally friendly**.

In brief

It is in the interests of businesses to reduce environmental problems. Environmental policies are often built into the aims and objectives of the business, to demonstrate what businesses call **corporate social responsibility** or CSR. Acting in an environmentally responsible way is often attractive to customers, so it helps to create and maintain customer loyalty. The government has also passed laws to make sure that businesses do not damage the environment or present a danger to communities.

Revision notes

- Many businesses aim to be environmentally responsible. This can bring advantages including greater efficiency and lower costs. For example, more fuel-efficient vehicles are both better for the environment and cheaper to run; removing excess packaging is better for the environment but also cuts costs.
- There is also likely to be increased custom that comes from having a better reputation. Being seen as environmentally friendly may be one of the main objectives of a business.

Dolphin-friendly tuna is caught in nets from which dolphins can escape — an example of a practice made environmentally friendly.

- The main environmental problems created by businesses are pollution (air, water, noise, visual, etc.) and waste products. These are called **social costs**. Some, such as traffic congestion, may be short-term and local. Others, such as carbon dioxide emissions, may be long-term and lead to international problems such as global warming.
- Many businesses also aim for sustainable production as, globally, resources decrease. This means ensuring that anything taken from the environment during production is replaced.
- Many businesses have recognised their impact on the local, national and world environment, and have taken steps to reduce this. The most common methods of reducing **carbon footprint** are:
  - recycling paper and packaging, and using recycled paper for packaging
  - only using timber from sustainable forests
  - fitting pollutant controls, such as smoke filters, wherever possible
  - using 'green' fuels in transport — usually meaning high performance in terms of kilometres per litre
  - fitting pollution-reduction devices such as catalytic converters
  - adopting energy-saving policies, such as lighting systems that switch on and off only when areas are in use

Speak the language

environmentally friendly — not harming the environment

corporate social responsibility (CSR) — business policy that is both ethically and environmentally responsible

social costs — costs that affect the whole community, such as pollution

carbon footprint — the amount of carbon released (and therefore environmental damage caused) through an activity

Ingram

Pollution is a major social cost created by businesses

In a nutshell

* Businesses should be friendly to the environment.
* An environmentally friendly approach is good for the business's reputation and customer loyalty.
* This means that such an approach often also makes good business sense.

Boost your grade You will gain more marks if you are clear that there are often dual benefits to being environmentally friendly. Policies may both reduce costs and increase customer loyalty.

Test yourself

Fill in the missing words from the list below. If you are feeling confident, cover the words and do the exercise from memory.

Businesses can bring both benefits and .... to the .... within which they operate. Although businesses may provide jobs, they may also cause ...., such as

....

Many businesses regulate themselves, to make sure that the bad effects of their business do not upset the .... Often they include environmental targets in their .... The advantages of being .... include greater .... and lower .... There is also the increased custom due to having a better ....

communities   costs   disadvantages   efficiency

environmentally friendly   local community   objectives

pollution   reputation   social costs

International trade

What the specification requires

You need to understand how and why international trade takes place and how economic issues impact on trade. You should be aware of how protection policies can harm trade. You should realise that governments sometimes resort to protecting home businesses from competition.

In brief

Without international trade, many of the products that we take for granted would not exist. International trade allows businesses to exchange goods that they can produce with those that businesses in other countries can produce. This benefits both parties as long as production takes place in the country that is relatively more efficient at producing that particular product. Globalisation describes the movement of businesses to operating on a worldwide basis. Some businesses make a point of focusing on global markets rather than on local ones.

Revision notes

- International trade is made up of two distinct types of product, moving in two directions. The types of product are **visibles**, which are goods that can be seen or touched, and **invisibles**, which are services such as insurance or transport that cannot be seen or touched.

- Products move either into or out of a country. **Imports** are products brought into a country from abroad, while **exports** are those sold to countries abroad.
- Income distribution globally is extremely uneven, with a few rich countries and many poor and very poor ones. Businesses may take advantage of these income inequalities to exploit

Cargoes are shipped around the world in containers

developing countries. For example, multinationals, with factories and operations in many countries, may be able to take advantage of lower labour costs, or less organised labour. This has brought globalisation into conflict with human rights groups, which see global businesses as exploiting labour or natural resources in poorer countries in order to boost profits in richer ones. Some businesses are criticised for this. Others are congratulated for bringing work to poorer countries.

■ Countries may try to protect home businesses by making imports more expensive through taxes or **tariffs**, or encouraging exports through **subsidies**. Such protection may be needed for developing countries, but it is also used by developed countries to protect, for example, employment.

■ This means that there are many ethical and political issues attached to international trade. Some see free trade (trade without export or import restrictions) as a force for good; others see it as destroying the chances of developing countries to compete.

In a nutshell

* International trade is generally seen as a good thing, providing countries with products they could not otherwise enjoy.
* Trade has its problems if businesses take advantage of the inequalities between developing and developed countries.
* Developing countries may therefore protect businesses to help them compete.
* UK businesses are affected by such protection. They may also find that new markets bring both threats and opportunities.

Speak the language

visibles — trade in goods

invisibles — trade in services

imports — products brought into a country from abroad

exports — products sent and sold abroad

tariffs — additional charges, such as a tax, put on imports

subsidies — money given to businesses to keep export prices low

Test yourself

Choose the most appropriate answer from each of the choices below.

1 If you were in the UK, a sale of cars to the USA would be **(a)** a visible export, **(b)** an invisible import, **(c)** a visible import, **(d)** an invisible export.

2 An amount of money given to an exported product to reduce its price is called **(a)** a tariff, **(b)** a subsidy, **(c)** a support payment, **(d)** an ethical payment.

3 If you lived in the UK and hired a car while on holiday in the USA, to the US economy this would be **(a)** a visible export, **(b)** an invisible import, **(c)** a visible import, **(d)** an invisible export.

4 Free trade means that international trade should **(a)** not cost anything to importers, **(b)** not be restricted by countries, **(c)** not cost anything to exporters, **(d)** not cost anything to consumers.

5 If you lived in the USA and bought a flight from Air France, this would be **(a)** a visible export, **(b)** an invisible import, **(c)** a visible import, **(d)** an invisible export.

6 Multinationals may be able to take advantage of less developed countries due to all of the following EXCEPT **(a)** lower labour costs, **(b)** less strict employment rules, **(c)** less strict safety rules, **(d)** lower population levels.

7 If you lived in the UK and bought goods from a US website, to the UK economy this would be **(a)** a visible export, **(b)** an invisible import, **(c)** a visible import, **(d)** an invisible export.

8 An amount added on to an imported product to increase its price is called **(a)** a tariff, **(b)** a subsidy, **(c)** a support payment, **(d)** an ethical payment.

9 One threat to the UK economy from international trade is **(a)** the emergence of new markets, **(b)** the emergence of new competitors, such as China, **(c)** a boost to growth at home, **(d)** a boost to growth abroad.

10 One possible benefit to the UK economy from international trade is **(a)** the emergence of new markets, **(b)** the emergence of new competitors, such as China, **(c)** a boost to growth at home, **(d)** a boost to growth abroad.

Boost your grade

AO2 to AO3: for top marks you should be able to discuss the opportunities and threats for UK businesses from trade and growth. For example, countries such as China, Brazil, South Korea and India have, in the twenty-first century, experienced 'supergrowth'. By contrast, many developed countries, including the UK, have suffered no or negative growth. UK businesses may therefore find new markets emerging, but also tougher competition.

Topic 44
The impact of government and the EU

What the specification requires

You need to understand why governments — at both national and international level — feel that they need to regulate businesses. You should realise that many regulations add to the costs of businesses, and may therefore be resisted, but that many are seen as vital by groups such as employees and consumers.

In brief

Businesses are regulated by national and international governments. Many regulations add to the costs of businesses but are for the benefit of employees and customers. In particular, in the UK, businesses must conform to British government and European Union (EU) regulations. These include health-and-safety and consumer protection legislation as well as laws designed to promote the fair and equal treatment of employees, such as anti-discrimination legislation. Businesses also have to pay taxes to the government.

Revision notes

- The UK government passes laws and regulations, many of which affect businesses. Many encourage fair treatment of workers, such as race and gender equality legislation and equal-pay Acts. The UK is also a member of the **European Union** (EU).
- The EU is a group of countries in Europe that have agreed to act together on a number of issues, many of which affect business. This provides businesses within the EU with a larger market (the **single European market**) of over 360 million people. The EU has over

two dozen member states and stretches from Sweden and Finland in the north to Malta and Greece in the south, from Portugal and Spain in the west to Latvia and Estonia in the east. It is a powerful trading bloc that other countries are keen to join.

> **Speak the language**
>
> **European Union (EU)** — the countries of Europe that have joined together to make trade and employment easier, and to compete internationally
>
> **single European market** — the population of the EU considered as one market
>
> **Maastricht Treaty** — the treaty that took a big step in getting all EU countries to agree to similar standards and benefits, especially for workers

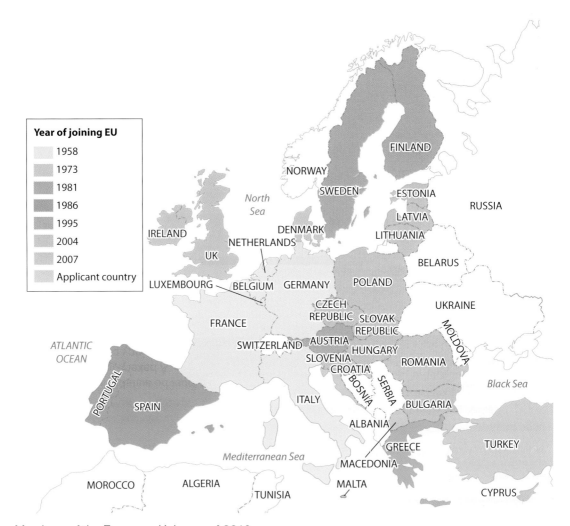

Members of the European Union as of 2010

- The **Maastricht Treaty** of 1991 was designed to encourage all member states to work within the same rules. It included the Social Chapter, which promoted:
  - the right for workers to join a trade union
  - the right to equal treatment for men and women at work
  - more worker involvement in businesses through worker councils
  - a minimum wage
  - maximum working hours
  - freedom for EU citizens to work in any EU country
- Each policy has benefits and drawbacks. For example, the minimum wage ensures fair treatment but increases costs; the right to work anywhere in the UK could mean workers arriving in the UK from poorer countries, leading to unemployment among those already resident.
- Many businesses would argue that some regulation (such as health and safety) is vital, but that many regulations are an unwanted restriction.

In a nutshell

* Businesses are both taxed and regulated.
* In the UK, most regulation comes from either the government or the EU.
* Much regulation is for the protection and fair treatment of employees and consumers.
* Regulation can add to the costs of businesses.
* Some regulations may be seen by businesses as unnecessary 'red tape'.

Test yourself

State whether each of the following statements is true or false.

1 The UK government passes laws and regulations that may affect businesses.

2 UK employment law covers areas such as discrimination, equality and fair treatment.

3 The European Union is a group of European countries that have decided to act together, especially in areas like trade.

4 The 'single European market' refers to the market within a single EU country.

5 The Social Chapter gives workers the right to work in any EU country.

6 The minimum wage decreases the costs of business.

7 The EU will not expand any further as no other country wishes to join.

8 The UK is a member of the European Union.

9 The Maastricht Treaty lays down different rules for different member states.

10 The EU promises workers more say in businesses through worker councils.

AO2: for AO2 marks, you would be expected to be able to apply your knowledge. You should therefore be able to talk about the effect of laws on a particular business. For example, what would be the consequences for the business if there were no health-and-safety legislation?

Section test: External influences on business

1 'Ethics' is best described as
   (a) making a profit
   (b) doing the right thing
   (c) having standards
   (d) producing a lot

2 Examples of ethical practice include all of the following except:
   (a) not testing products on animals
   (b) using cheap labour
   (c) paying fair prices for materials
   (d) not producing goods under dangerous conditions

3 Businesses may be keen to act ethically because:
   (a) it improves their reputation
   (b) it improves their profits
   (c) it leads to lower costs
   (d) it keeps more people employed

4 Which of the following is NOT a pressure group?
   (a) PETA
   (b) WWF
   (c) BBC
   (d) Greenpeace

5 CSR stands for:
   (a) corporate social risk
   (b) company social responsibility
   (c) corporate special responsibility
   (d) corporate social responsibility

6 Social costs include which of the following: (i) traffic jams, (ii) air pollution, (iii) noisy factory operations, (iv) carbon dioxide emissions?
   (a) (i) only
   (b) (i) and (ii) only
   (c) (i) and (iii)
   (d) all of these

7 Goods bought from abroad that can be seen and touched are called:
   (a) invisible imports
   (b) visible exports
   (c) visible imports
   (d) invisible exports

8 The Single Market has approximately how many people in it?
   (a) 0.36 million
   (b) 3.6 million
   (c) 36 million
   (d) 360 million

9 EU stands for:
   (a) European Universe
   (b) European Union
   (c) Europe United
   (d) Europes Union

10 Restrictions on international trade include which of the following: (i) tariffs, (ii) costs, (iii) subsidies, (iv) exports?
   (a) (i) only
   (b) (i) and (ii) only
   (c) (i) and (iii) only
   (d) all of these

Practice exam

The Edexcel paper for this part of the specification lasts for 90 minutes. It is divided into three sections.

Section A

Answer all the questions in this section.

You should spend 40 minutes on this section.

1 (a) The Boston matrix shows the performance of the range of products made and sold by a business. This range of products is usually referred to by the term (choose one option):
- product trial
- product matrix
- product range
- product differentiation
- product portfolio   *(1 mark)*

(b) Describe the key characteristics of the four types of product shown in the matrix below.   *(8 marks)*

(c) Explain why the Boston matrix is a valuable tool for a business   *(3 marks)*

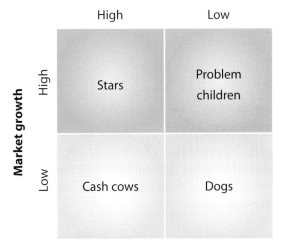

Market share

2 (a) PetsFirst sells a range of specialist pet foods and pet accessories. The business wants to encourage repeat purchases so has set up a focus group to see what customers think of its range.

This is an example of which of the following? (Choose one option.)

- quantitative research
- secondary research
- statistical research
- qualitative research
- desk research *(1 mark)*

(b) Explain why PetsFirst wants to encourage repeat purchases. *(3 marks)*

(c) The owners of PetsFirst have discussed the following methods of promoting the business:

- providing a 'buy three products and the lowest-priced one is free' offer
- selling other products, such as cat and dog flaps and birdcages
- providing a 'satisfaction or your money back' guarantee
- providing a monthly newsletter to customers

Recommend which TWO of these would be most effective in promoting the business. Give reasons for your recommendation. *(8 marks)*

3 (a) White's is a chain of high street shops, selling clothes, food and household goods. Recently, the business introduced a new range of 'Quality Mark' branded foods. When launched, they were priced at less than it cost to produce them.

This is an example of which of the following pricing strategies? (Choose one option.)

- cost-plus pricing
- penetration pricing
- loss leader
- skimming
- mark-up pricing *(1 mark)*

(b) Explain how 'Quality Mark' could help White's to compete. *(3 marks)*

(c) Suggest TWO other ways in which White's could be more competitive. *(4 marks)*

4 (a) Sarah is setting up a hairdressing business. She has employed one full-time member of staff to work during the week and three part-time staff. She pays them for the hours they work. This is an example of which of the following? (Choose one.)

- piece rate
- salary
- commission
- time rate
- overtime rate *(1 mark)*

(b) **Explain why Sarah might have decided to employ both full-time and part-time staff.** *(3 marks)*

(c) **Explain how motivating the staff could lead to higher profitability.** *(4 marks)*

Total: 40 marks

Section B

You should spend 30 minutes on this section.

Read the passage and answer the questions.

Jayne Hepplethwaite and Anjum Khan have been working in the clothing and fashion business for over 5 years. Jayne has a degree in fashion design and has worked for some of the top fashion houses. Anjum is a fashion writer, with a degree in journalism. Recently, they decided to set up their own business. They will produce hand-made silk scarves, as they have spotted a gap in the market.

Jayne and Anjum decided that their fixed costs in the first year would be £20,000. The variable cost per scarf is £15 and the scarves would be priced at £25 each.

5 (a) **Define what is meant by breakeven sales.** *(3 marks)*

(b) **Explain how using breakeven can help Jayne and Anjum with their business planning.** *(4 marks)*

(c) **Calculate their breakeven in the first year of operation. Show your working.** *(8 marks)*

(d) **Anjum thinks that £25 is too high a price for the scarves. Calculate breakeven if they lowered the price to £20. Show your working.** *(6 marks)*

(e) **Explain how Jayne and Anjum could improve the profitability of their scarves.** *(4 marks)*

6 **One customer bought a scarf and found it did not keep her warm. Nevertheless, all her friends admired it. Explain why customers still buy Jayne and Anjum's scarves even though they do not keep them warm.** *(6 marks)*

Total: 30 marks

Section C

You should spend 20 minutes on this section.

Read the passage and answer the questions that follow.

Getafone is one of the newest players in the UK mobile phone market, but is rapidly taking market share because of its concerns for the environment. Mobile phones are made from many different materials, including zinc and aluminium, both of which are often mined under terrible working conditions. Getafone has ethical policies in place to make sure that none of the components of its phones comes from such sources.

Getafone is an American company that sells phones internationally. As its CEO, Matt Finlay, says, 'Getafone believes that free trade will benefit both developed and developing nations equally.' In its latest corporate report, Getafone has promised to reduce the carbon footprint per phone by at least 25% by 2015.

7 (a) **Explain what is meant by the term 'carbon footprint'.** *(2 marks)*

   (b) **Suggest and explain FOUR ways by which Getafone could reduce its carbon footprint.** *(8 marks)*

   (c) **Recommend one of the ways which you have suggested as the best way for this business. Give reasons for your recommendation.** *(6 marks)*

8 **Explain the advantages and disadvantages of free trade for each of the following.**

   (a) **emerging nations**

   (b) **established trading nations** *(4 marks)*

Total: 20 marks

Controlled assessment

Introduction and general advice

Controlled assessment is a new type of assessment that is replacing coursework. It tests the same sort of skills as coursework used to test, but under conditions that are more controlled. Controlled assessments are designed to be:

- researched independently
- completed during lessons within a set time
- supervised during the final write-up

There is a recommended time for research and for final write-up for each assessment.

This means that, with most assessments, you can undertake the research at home, or in a library, or on the internet. You can take a folder or portfolio of your research into the classroom when you are doing your final write-up.

You should choose one of the tasks that are set. Your teacher can give you feedback on your choice of task, on the focus you have chosen and on the sort of research that you are undertaking. This must all take place before the final write-up.

The final stage is a supervised period to write up your research findings. This can be spread across a number of sessions. You are advised to spend around 6 hours on the research and 3 hours on the write-up. Your teacher will supervise this stage.

The controlled assessment unit you attempt will depend on the qualification route you have decided. If you are taking the full course, you will take Unit 2: Investigating small businesses.

Advice on Unit 2: Investigating small business

The content on which you will be assessed for Unit 2 is the same as that for Unit 1. You are just tested on it in a different way.

You will be asked to select one task from a list provided by Edexcel, which will change from time to time. You are advised to spend around 6 hours researching the task and then around 3 hours writing it up. You can carry out your research in your school or college, or at home. You can take the results of your research into the writing-up session. When you write up the task, you will be supervised by your teacher and must work on your own. You will receive marks for the way you demonstrate research skills, presentation skills, analysis (or presentation of an argument) and evaluation (or conclusions drawn, judgements made and recommendations given).

The tasks in the first year of the qualification give a good indication of the types of task that will be set in future years.

Task 1 looks at what qualities of an entrepreneur are most important in making a success of a business. It is suggested that you might wish to interview an entrepreneur or construct a questionnaire to ask of one or more entrepreneurs.

Task 2 asks you to choose a business that has competitors in your local area and research how it competes with these rival businesses.

Task 3 asks you to choose a local business and investigate how it motivates its workers.

Task 4 asks you to choose a local business and investigate the way in which it uses the marketing mix. You should be able to draw conclusions about which part of the mix is the most important to this business.

Task 5 asks you to choose a local business that has been affected by changes in interest rates recently, and to assess how these changes have impacted on the business.

At the highest level, you will be awarded marks for:
- detailed, relevant research from a wide range of sources
- good organisation of materials
- a clear focus to your investigation
- collection and use of appropriate data
- presentation of information accurately and in a range of appropriate formats
- detailed and relevant analysis of material, weighing up both sides of an argument
- relevant and clear judgements and supported conclusions, using the evidence collected

Other examined Edexcel units

Advice on Unit 4: Business communications

Unit 4, taken with Units 1 and 2, forms the Business Communications GCSE. There are four topic areas in this unit:

- Communication
- Communication with stakeholders of a business
- Business communication tools
- Communication via the web

Communication

This topic looks at the traditional model of communication: sender, message, medium, receiver, feedback. It investigates the purpose of communication and its particular importance in a business context. It studies the different types of communication that may be used in different contexts both within businesses and between businesses and their customers. It recognises that there can be barriers to communication and considers how these may be overcome to ensure efficient business communication. This topic also looks at the consequences and benefits of good and bad business communication.

Communication with stakeholders of a business

Both internal and external stakeholders need to receive messages sent from a business to them. These messages may be sent by a variety of means, including oral, written, electronic and visual methods. The topic notes that web- and electronically-based media are increasingly important, but that traditional media, such as note-taking at meetings, still have their place. The topic looks in detail at how various communications should be constructed and who are the appropriate groups when using each.

Business communication tools

This topic looks at the skills that are needed for business communication, such as word-processing, emails, presentation techniques and desktop publishing. It also looks at 'cutting-edge' types of business communication, such as videoconferencing and teleconferencing. This topic also discusses the way in which a business may be structured, and the impact this has on its various communications channels.

Communication via the web

The focus of this topic is on how a business can best use the internet, or world wide web, to communicate. It looks at the advantages and disadvantages of having an online presence such as a website, and at some of the technicalities of creating and maintaining sites. The features that a business should have on its website are also considered. The legal rights and responsibilities of those hosting, running and using websites are all part of this topic area.

Advice on Unit 5: Introduction to economic understanding

Unit 5, taken with Units 1 and 2, forms the Business Studies and Economics GCSE. There are five topic areas in this unit:

■ How can I start to think like an economist?
■ Risk or certainty?
■ Big or small?
■ Is growth good?
■ Is the world fair?

How can I start to think like an economist?

This topic is where you will study the basic truths that form the basis for the study of economics. The topic looks at choice, and the consequences of making a choice in terms of opportunity cost. It looks at how price changes impact on sales and why they may not always work in the way predicted by a business, including the concept of price elasticity. The topic looks at the different outcomes or aspects that each stakeholder in a business would wish to see, and how these might conflict, and also at the hidden costs and benefits of decisions.

Risk or certainty?

This topic covers how decisions are based on a calculation of risk and how such risk can be minimised. In particular, there is a focus on business success or failure. The ways of measuring success are considered, as are the causes and measures of failure. The success or failure of an economy can also be measured, so this topic looks at problems and issues in economies (e.g. inflation and unemployment) and at variables that will affect these (e.g. exchange rates and interest rates).

Big or small?

In this area you will study the relative strengths and weaknesses of large and small businesses. Both how businesses grow and why they grow are studied. The growth of a business to a point where it has monopoly power is considered, and whether this is a good or bad thing (for both the business and society as a whole). The topic also considers whether big business can be trusted to regulate itself, or whether there should be other forms of regulation, such as from competition authorities, the government and the European Union. The influence and effect of pressure groups is also studied.

Is growth good?

This topic looks at growth and considers both its costs and benefits. Economic growth and the ways in which it is measured are defined, and the factors that cause growth are discussed. The topic looks at the various measures of standard of living in a country and considers that growth is only one of those measures. It also looks at the possible negative effects of growth and whether, in the long term, economies can expect just to keep on growing indefinitely. The ways in which governments regulate economies and trade to encourage growth and discourage negative effects form part of this section.

Is the world fair?

The main focus in this final topic area is on the way that countries — and their populations — are unequal. It looks at types of inequality and at how governments and trade might be able to iron out at least some of the differences. The efforts of national and international businesses, governments and other organisations such as charities are investigated.

Advice on Unit 6: Introduction to small business

If you are taking the short course, you will take Unit 6: Introduction to small business.

Unit 6 is assessed by a single examination, consisting of multiple-choice and short-answer questions. The content for Unit 6 is the same as Unit 1.

Speak the language index

A HISTORY of
ST. JOHN'S, BRIGHTON

SHIRE PUBLICATIONS

A HISTORY *of*
ST. JOHN'S, BRIGHTON

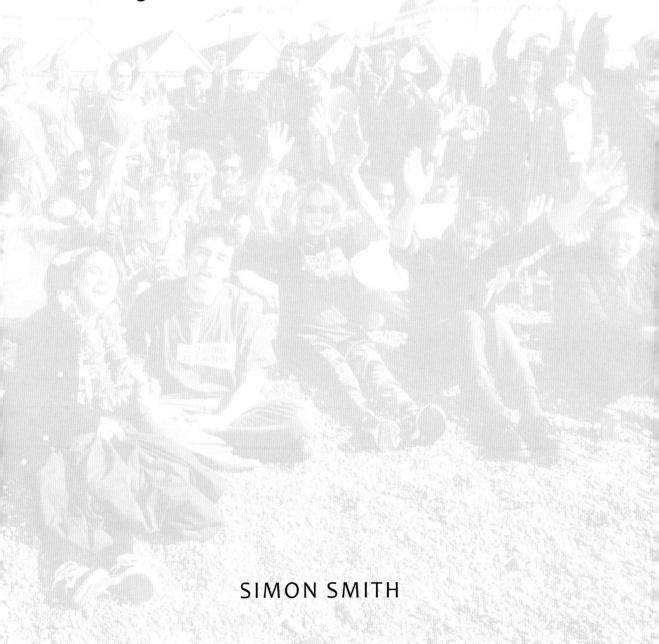

SIMON SMITH

SHIRE PUBLICATIONS

Bloomsbury Publishing Plc
PO Box 883, Oxford, OX1 9PL, UK
1385 Broadway, 5th Floor, New York, NY 10018, USA

E-mail: shire@bloomsbury.com
www.shirebooks.co.uk

SHIRE is a trademark of Osprey Publishing Ltd

First published in Great Britain in 2018

A catalogue record for this book is available from the British Library.

ISBN: PB 978 1 78442 347 6
         eBook ISBN: 978 1 78442 348 3
         ePDF ISBN: 978 1 78442 345 2
         XML ISBN: 978 1 78442 346 9

18 19 20 21 22   10 9 8 7 6 5 4 3 2 1

Index by Sandra Shotter

Cover and page layouts by Myriam Bell Design, Shrewsbury, UK
Printed and bound by Bell & Bain Ltd., Glasgow G46 7UQ

Shire Publications supports the Woodland Trust, the UK's leading woodland conservation charity. Between 2014 and 2018 our donations are being spent on their Centenary Woods project in the UK.

Cover image
The south-east front of St. John's by Jay Collins. (With thanks to the artist)

Half title page image
(St. John's College)

Title page image
(Terry Applin Photographer)

Page 10 image
Sister Jane with her cat and pupils in 1890. This is the earliest known group photograph of the Home. (St. John's College)

Back cover image
(St. John's College)

Contents

Acknowledgements

MANY PEOPLE HAVE contributed to this project: Lavender Jones, whose capacity for combing through census returns and online sleuthing has done much to illuminate the early years of St. John's Home; Sister Mary Julian of the Community of the Holy Cross, whose help with the history of the Community, supply of photographs and knowledge of the life of Jane Borradaile, has been invaluable; and Ann, whose personal reminiscences of life as a convalescent in 1951 have enlivened the book.

At St. John's, I always appreciate the warm welcome from the helpful Reception staff at the College, for which I am very thankful. I would also like to thank Lucy Howells, Marketing Manager, for keeping me on my toes and facilitating so many meetings and unearthing material, Naomi Alder (the CEO's PA), Rachel Llewellyn and Liz Coles. My gratitude also goes to Mark Ryan for his extensive help with archive material and with the recent history of St. John's; Dennis Boxall for talking so helpfully about his 23 years at St. John's; Sharon Jaque, a former member of staff at St. John's; Julie Bolton at Seaford; Shelagh Heath for her recollections of her 27 years as Finance Manager; and Richard Stewart, Chairman of the Trustees, Len Parkyn, Chairman of the Governors and a Trustee, Jean Marshall, a Trustee, and Julie Newson (former Head of Care, Borradaile, who is now Deacon of St Luke's) for sharing with me their collective experiences of St. John's.

My appreciation also goes to Les Crawley and Tony Cowie for their insight into the dog shows; Oliver Smyth for his help with electrical treatments; the ever-helpful staff at The Keep; Lynn Painter for the photograph of Whitehanger, near Haslemere; and Matthew Barrett, his mother and neighbours for casting light on St. John's evacuation to Muntham in 1941–42. Above all, I am hugely grateful to Anita Baker for her assiduous editing.

Opposite: Panorama of Brighton from the gardens of St. John's. (St. John's College)

Foreword

SOME OF MY happiest moments during my many years involved with autism have been spent while visiting the schools and colleges that support young people living with this very complex and potentially devastating condition, and the visits I've made to St. John's are without doubt some of my highlights.

This fascinating history makes clear that although the approach to and methods of helping vulnerable young people at St. John's may have changed, the ethos and caring approach that lie behind them have always existed, from the early beginnings as a convalescent home helping victims of deprivation in Victorian England through to its current status as a nationally acknowledged centre for those with autism and other related conditions.

The problems that beset our children and young adults at St. John's are different nowadays, to be sure: coping with the physical diseases that were commonplace in Victorian England – diphtheria, scarlet fever, whooping cough, polio, tetanus and typhoid – has given way to caring for those who need support for more subtle difficulties. However, the need for the professional and humane approach that has always been the hallmark of the staff is as strong as ever.

Illustrated throughout with photographs, maps, posters, programmes and other memorabilia, this comprehensive book is a historical document in its own right, but, much more, is a testament to the ongoing need for wonderful institutions such as St. John's and the standard of care that it provides. Long may it survive, and continue its important work.

Jane Asher

Jane Asher
President, National Autistic Society

Jane Asher opening Scrummies on 23 October 2013. (St. John's College)

Part I

St. John's Convalescent Home: A History

Chapter 1

Is there really such a place?

IN DICKENS' LAST completed novel, *Our Mutual Friend* (1865), the elderly Betty Higden is concerned about her ailing little grandson Johnny. His breathing is difficult. 'Me choking, granny,' he says from his grandmother's lap.

He is clearly in urgent need of medical attention, which his family know to be expensive. The kindly John Rokesmith suggests taking him to 'a place where there are none but children; a place set up on purpose for sick children; where the good doctors and nurses pass their lives with children, talk to none but children, touch none but children, comfort and cure none but children.'

'Is there really such a place?' asked the old woman with a gaze of wonder?

'Yes, Betty, on my word and you shall see it.'[1]

The place Johnny is taken to is 'The Children's Hospital', what we now know as Great Ormond Street Hospital for Sick Children, founded in 1852, just three years before the novel appeared.

Once there, Johnny was 'to find himself lying in a quiet little bed…and at the bed's head was a coloured picture, beautiful to see, representing as it were another Johnny seated on the knee of some Angel surely who loved little children. And, marvellous fact, to lie and stare at: Johnny had become one of a little family, all in little quiet beds…with little platforms whereon were to be

1   Dickens, Charles, *Our Mutual Friend* (OUP, 1952), p328

Left: The original Hospital for Sick Children at 49 Great Ormond Street, c. 1870. (Archive Service, Great Ormond Street Hospital for Children NHS Foundation Trust)

Right: The Aunt Judy Cot, sponsored in 1868 by the eponymous children's magazine, and the first such endowed cot there. This is the sort of cot Johnny would have found himself in. Sister Jane was active in having cots and beds endowed at St. John's. (Archive Service, Great Ormond Street Hospital for Children NHS Foundation Trust)

Sardonyx representation of Florence Nightingale (1820–1910), nurse and reformer, by Luigi Saulini, 1855–60. (Metropolitan Museum of Art, NY)

seen dolls' houses, woolly dogs with mechanical barks…tin armies, Moorish tumblers, wooden tea things, and the riches of the earth.'[2] Sadly, Johnny's illness, presumably tuberculosis, is too far gone and the chapter ends with a deathbed scene.

Johnny's plight and John Rokesmith's attempts to help him provide an apt illustration in fiction of GM Trevelyan's assertion in his *English Social History* that 'An enlarged sympathy with children was one of the chief contributions made by the Victorian English to real civilisation'. It also of course illustrates Dickens' role in exposing the plight of children and engaging his readers' sympathies. Whilst modern readers may find this scene and others like it sentimental, there can be no doubt as to its effectiveness. More than this, Johnny's condition has come about through exposure to the appalling living conditions that were to be found in poor quarters of all large cities, where the air was foul, the atmosphere damp, the water poor and the food meagre.

In short, Victorian London was not a healthy place, nor was any town centre in the industrial age. Children suffered from multiple influenza outbreaks, diphtheria, scarlet fever, measles, whooping cough, polio, tetanus, and typhoid. Merely keeping sanitary was difficult until the later ages of piped water. This, combined with the lack of vaccinations for diseases, led to an extremely high infant mortality rate amongst all classes of society. Mortality rates for the 1860s and 70s provide stark evidence of the harmful effects of polluted air and harsh living conditions. For example, the average life span in 1840, in the Whitechapel district of

2   Dickens, Charles, *Our Mutual Friend* (OUP, 1952), p330

London, was 45 years for the upper class and 27 years for tradesmen. Labourers and servants lived only 22 years on average.

Infant and child mortality was shockingly high. The plight of Johnny is uncannily echoed by Katherine Mansfield 70 years later in her short story, 'The Life of Ma Parker'. Again, a grandmother, Ma Parker herself, remembers the suffering of her grandson Lennie while going about her work of drudgery. She recalls the bogus remedies she sends off postal orders to buy in order that Lennie might be relieved of his cough.

> From Lennie's little box of a chest there came a sound as though something was boiling. There was a great lump of something bubbling in his chest that he couldn't get rid of. When he coughed the sweat sprang out on his head; his eyes bulged, his hands waved, and the great lump bubbled as a potato knocks in a saucepan.[3]

Her employer, 'the literary gentleman', is no John Rokesmith, but one who totally fails to understand the pain of his charwoman's loss, let alone the agony of Lennie's condition. What a difference proper nursing, valid medication and, above all, clean air would have made to both Johnny and Lennie.

In the 1860s, Florence Nightingale brought more attention to the use of ventilation and site selection in preventing disease in hospitals. Her *Notes on Nursing: What it is and What it is Not*, published in 1859 and still in print today, proved to be a seminal work. Her experiences in the Crimea showed her that many more men died from infection and poor hygiene than from their wounds. Cleanliness, ventilation, clean bedding, nutritious food and rigorous observation lay at the heart of nursing. She declared that a convalescent home was superior to hospital because of its healthful location and the change it provided from the dreary institutional life of hospital wards. These places would provide the domesticity of a home. 'As long as they are hospital inmates, they feel as hospital inmates, they think as hospital inmates, they act as hospital inmates, not as people recovering.'[4] In a pamphlet for one convalescent home of the period we

Brighton Blind Asylum, Eastern Road, now demolished. (With thanks to the Regency Society)

---

3   Mansfield, Katherine, *Garden Party and Other Stories* (Constable, 1922)

4   Nightingale, F., *Notes on Nursing: What it is and What it is Not* (Harrison of Pall Mall, 1859), p107

read that it provides '…tiny sufferers with relief from the stifling courts and slums of London and big cities'.[5]

It was thus that convalescent homes came to be built on the south coast in the 1870s and 80s in Broadstairs, Herne Bay, Margate, Ramsgate, Bognor and Brighton. Brighton, unlike London, was a famously heathy place, and had been so since Dr John Russell first advertised its health-giving properties in the 1740s. It also had a long history of providing educational institutions, including specialist schools. Over 150 schools feature in the Street Directories for 1848, and that year saw the publication of Dickens' *Dombey and Son*. The delicate Paul Dombey is sent away to school at Dr Blimber's Academy, high up on the cliff, a school popularly supposed to be based on Chichester House in Kemp Town.

5   Anders, Eli, *Locating Convalescence in Victorian England*, 7 November 2014.

Fresh air is good for you

Florence Nightingale in her influential manuals of the early 1860s, *Notes on Nursing* and *Notes on Hospitals*,[1] had much to say about the benefits of fresh air as an aid to recovery (see page 13). When The Hospital for Sick Children on Great Ormond Street in London opened in 1852 it had a large garden (now built over) and also rented outside space from the nearby Foundling Hospital in Lamb's Conduit Field in Bloomsbury. Patients were encouraged to spend as much time as possible there and these open spaces effectively became the convalescent wards of the hospital. When GOSH needed to expand and the green spaces were

1   Nightingale, F, *Notes on Hospitals* (Longman, Roberts and Green, 1863)

A balcony of the first purpose-built hospital building, opened in 1875. The photograph appears to have been taken in the 1920s, though the nurses' uniforms might have come from a much earlier age. (Archive Service, Great Ormond Street Hospital for Children NHS Foundation Trust)

Open air classes at St. John's, 1951. The balcony was sited on the top of the south side of the building, to the left of the gable. (St. John's College)

More rooted in reality, St Mary's Hall, founded by the Rev Henry Venn Elliott in 1836 for the daughters of clergy, and Brighton College, founded in 1845, were both in Eastern Road. Near them was the Brighton Institution for the Instruction of the Deaf and Dumb, which was founded in Egremont Place in 1841, and moved to Eastern Road, directly opposite Brighton College in 1848. Similarly, the Brighton Blind Asylum was founded in Queen's Road in 1841 and moved to a site on Eastern Road in 1881, on land given by the Rev Henry Venn Elliott. Its fine Venetian Gothic exterior by George Somers Clarke was a distinctive feature of the junction of Eastern Road and Bristol Gate. It closed in 1952 and was demolished six years later to make way for a hospital development, which has itself now been demolished as the Royal Sussex County Hospital undergoes a major rebuilding programme. Another 19th-century institution that was also annexed by the hospital was the Home for Female Orphans, just to the west of the Blind Asylum, which became Latilla House.

inevitably built over, beds were wheeled onto the balconies that ran the length of the hospital.

The open-air principle had also been advocated by the Metropolitan Asylums Board, which was responsible for hospitalising pupils who had contracted notifiable diseases, the most prevalent being smallpox (see Ann's account on pages 48–50).

The early years of St. John's Home were marked by an emphasis on the efficacies of fresh air. Well into the 1950s lessons were taken on the south-facing balcony throughout the year, and shelters were erected in the playground to enable children to sit there in all weathers. Whereas modern parents might be wary of allowing their children to 'catch their death of cold', it was accepted that this was part of healthy living for the young, in much the same way as it was commonplace for babies to be left outside in their prams in all weathers.

A *British Medical Journal* article from July 1898 advises that open-air sanatoria for tuberculosis sufferers should be situated 'where the prevailing winds sweep over the sea, or over moorland, or better still where these two features are associated, and fresh, pure air comes from all quarters of the compass'.

Those who have climbed to the top of Walpole Road to St. John's cannot fail to be struck by its unique position, with the racecourse above and the sea below. Of course, it was not just the air that the children breathed during their two- or three-month stay that improved their health; the exercise they took daily also helped to restore them.

St. John's playground, 1890s. Note the cumbersome swings and shelters in the background. This area is now the St. John's car park. (St. John's College)

Chapter 2

An entirely free home

A FREE SEASIDE convalescent home had its first mention in an open letter of March 1875 which was appealing for funds. 'I put forward no fresh plea as to the necessity of such institutions', the writer begins, using a cunning rhetorical device to intensify the urgency of the need for her scheme. She emphasises that this is to be a free home to benefit those children who would otherwise die of consumption. There was a steely determination for this enterprise to become a reality. Funds were required to furnish it and then maintain it, some of which had been found already. She goes on to name 14 gentlemen to whom enquiries may be made, including two members of her own family. This was a woman who meant business, indeed a shrewd businesswoman who had all the hallmarks of a persuasive and successful fund-raiser. Her name was Sister Jane Borradaile, and she would be the very lifeblood of St. John's for the next 43 years.

Jane Borradaile was born on 13 October 1825 at 34 Fenchurch Street, London. Her parents were John Watson Borradaile (a merchant) and Ann Stevens. Her paternal grandfather William was from Wigton in Cumbia and became High Sheriff for the county of Surrey, having married Ann Delapierre, daughter of the French Ambassador. The baptismal register of the parish of St Gabriel, Fenchurch, tells us that Jane was christened on 5 December 1825 by the Rev William Borradaile, her uncle, who himself has a memorial in St Andrew's Church, Hove, alongside one to his mother, erected after his death in 1865 at the age of 66. Jane was part of a large family; we know that by 1841 she had eight siblings, four of whom survived into adulthood. She had three younger sisters, Emma, Grace and Harriet, none of whom married, and a younger brother Thomas.

The path she followed that led to her becoming Sister Jane is not at all clear. We do know that for most

William Borradaile's monument in St Andrew's, Hove. William was Jane's uncle; Elizabeth and Thomas her grandparents. Although Jane's childhood was spent in London, Brighton and Hove would have been familiar to her.

of her life she was associated with the Community of the Holy Cross (see pages 18–19), an Anglican order of nuns, originally working in the East End, that in due course adopted the Rule of St Benedict. It is possible that she entered the Community as early as the year of its foundation in 1857, when she was 32. We know that in 1866 there was a cholera epidemic in the East End, and the Sisters worked tirelessly among the sick and dying. Elizabeth Neale,[6] the founder of the Community, wrote: 'We used to cook for and distribute food to numbers varying between 100 and 300, and one room in our house was given up as a refuge, to which the infants of those sick or dead of the cholera could immediately be brought.' Sister Mary Julian, Superior of the order today, suggests that the sight of so many sick and dying children must have had a lasting influence on Jane and the experience may well have been the impetus to begin her lifelong work. Sister Jane is recorded as a Postulant on 1 January 1873. She then became the Community's first Associate Sister in 1875. As she says in a letter of that year, the purpose of the Home was two-fold: 'partly for the use

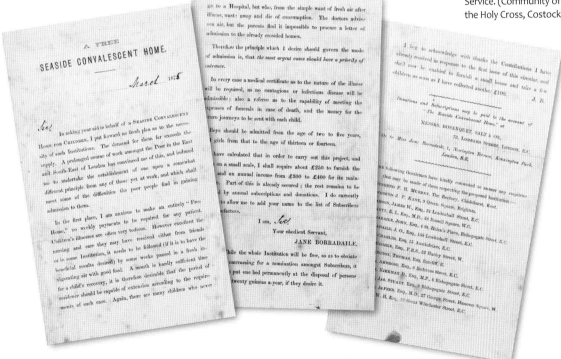

Sister Jane Borradaile (1825–1918), foundress of St. John's Home for Convalescent and Crippled Children also for Orphan Girls to be Trained for Domestic Service. (Community of the Holy Cross, Costock)

---

6   Elizabeth lived with her family in Hove until 1839, and founded a small orphanage, St Catherine's, there. It is interesting to speculate whether she and Jane ever met during the lost years before the founding of St John's in 1875.

Jane Borradaile's 1875 appeal letter. She had a steely determination to make this enterprise a reality. Despite this, it would be ten years before St. John's had a permanent, purpose-built home.

and relief of poor children recovering from severe illness or suffering from disease brought on by poverty and neglect; partly as a home for poor or homeless children with a view to training them for domestic service or some other useful career.'

The Home had a number of bases in Kemp Town before it was able finally to move into purpose-built premises in Walpole Road. The first of these was a small house, 9 Sudeley Place, just below the Royal Sussex County Hospital. There were five children there. We know from notes kept at the Convent of the Holy Cross that Sister Jane would take the children who came to stay in the house down to the beach, 'where she would write innumerable letters begging for financial help to carry out her desires'. A further lease of 1881 shows us that she moved the Home to 12 and 13 College Road, a short distance to the west, just below Brighton College. The relative size of the new property shows that the enterprise was expanding.

The Community of the Holy Cross

The Community that included Sister Jane amongst its number has its origins in the East End. Father Charles Fuge Lowder (1820–80) was a missionary priest working from St George-in-the-East in the London Docks. He was a high churchman, who was part of the Anglo Catholic revival in England and whose 'Roman rituals and vestments' provoked public outrage and even riots. Realising that there was much mission work to be done in the area, Lowder invited Elizabeth Neale (the sister of John Mason Neale, the hymn writer) to undertake that work in 1857 and she accordingly founded a Community of Sisters.

This work in London Docks was certainly not for the fainthearted; there was much child poverty, and a high proportion of petty criminals, prostitutes and thus unwanted children. It is a mark of Elizabeth Neale's commitment that she accepted and pursued the challenge so readily.

Within the mission area, Lowder established the new parish of St Peter's, London Docks, in Wapping

Below, left: Father Charles Fuge Lowder (1820–80). He is credited with being the first Anglican clergyman to be called 'Father'. (Community of the Holy Cross, Costock)

Below, right: Nuns with children at St Stephen's Home, Haywards Heath. (Community of the Holy Cross, Costock)

In her 7th Annual Report, for 1881, the earliest one available, Sister Jane describes the distinguishing characteristics of what is now known as St. John's Convalescent Home:

> At first it was an ordinary Convalescent Home, accommodating 25 children remaining for a few weeks at a time; but I soon found I had to deal constantly with delicate children who required a lengthened residence by the sea if they were ever to be fit for the hard work of life. I have therefore decided, while retaining 7 or 8 beds for common convalescent cases, to keep some of the children as permanent inmates through the critical years of delicate childhood, giving them the 2 or 3 years of good food and pure sea air, which so often means restoration for life. The children are tended, taught and trained by ladies,

Lane. The church was built in 1866, in a 'muscular' architectural style, according to Pevsner. A clergy house was part of the building, and much later, in 1885 in Father Wainright's time, the large clergy house was divided into two to allow the Sisters better accommodation than their cramped and poor conditions in Calvert Street.

In the 1871 census Sister Jane appears at 2 Newington Terrace, Walworth. She is described as a 'visitor' so it seems probable that she was continuing to work alongside the Sisters, although at that time not a formal member of the Community.

The Community moved to its new Mother House in Haywards Heath in 1886 (the same year that Sister Jane moved into her new home in Walpole Road), where it remained for nearly 100 years. From 1920 until 1937 the Sisters were directly involved in the running of St. John's, caring for and educating the children who spent time there. Meanwhile, work continued in the parish of St Peter's and other deprived areas in a number of cities and towns throughout England.

Later generations of Sisters felt that the Community was being called to a life of greater withdrawal, effectively away from the mission work, and in due course the Benedictine Office, and later the Rule of St Benedict, were adopted. In 1979 the Sisters moved to a house near Loughborough in the East Midlands and then to its present site nearby in 2011.

Some children in the East End in the early 1900s. Such children would have been looked after by the Community. (The Church of England Children's Society)

The purpose-built convent now stands in farmland with wide views over the surrounding countryside. Although a small Community, the Sisters have space in which they can share the atmosphere and silence of their Benedictine life with many others – Oblates, and Associates and people from local parishes, who come for Retreats and Quiet Days throughout the year. Together with this ministry of hospitality and that of worship, prayer and intercession, other work is undertaken, which includes writing for a variety of publications and a large postal apostolate. Conservation and care of the environment, to be enjoyed by the Sisters and visitors alike, is also an important aspect of life for the Community.

no servants being kept, but 5 or 6 little girls of 13 or 14 to help in the house. The ladies train them in household work, cooking and needlework, giving them sound religious instruction and simple teaching in reading and summing.

It is interesting that Sister Jane should make a virtue out of employing no servants, when in fact using the older children for domestic duties was an economic necessity, if she was to make ends meet. These days we would describe this particular part of the Home's purpose as vocational training, an aspect of St. John's work that continues to be

Dr Richard Hughes (1836–1902)

Dr Richard Hughes (1836–1902), a pioneer of homeopathic medicine.

In the same way that Sister Jane liked to attract the great and good to be subscribers and donors to her Home, and advertise their involvement, she liked to list on her prospectus and reports the names of eminent doctors and consulting physicians who would attend the children, presumably giving generously of their services. Notable amongst these, whilst the Home was in College Road, was Richard Hughes MD, MRCS, LRCP. He and his wife Sarah, herself the daughter of a Brighton doctor, lived at 5 College Place with their eight children, two of whom died in infancy. Richard's widowed father, Philip, also came to live with them on his retirement from the Treasury and War Office. It was, therefore, like Nos 12 and 13 just up the road, a busy household.

Apart from being a local doctor – he practised as a surgeon at the Brighton Orthopaedic Hospital – Richard Hughes was a pioneer in the field of homeopathic medicine. This system of treating sick people with small amounts of natural substances that would produce in well people the same effects as the diseases themselves was regarded with suspicion at this time, along with other forms of complementary or alternative medicine. However, it is a mark of Hughes' passion and influence that homeopathic treatments came to be seen as *bona fide* courses of action for a number of conditions, notably asthma.

His scholarly capacity led him to help Dr Dudgeon with the English translation of *Materia Medica Pura*, the great treatise on homeopathic medicine by the German physician Samuel Hahnemann (1755–1843). Indeed, he was present in 1898 when Hahnemann's body was exhumed 55 years after his death in order to be reinterred in Père Lachaise Cemetery in Paris beneath a monument more fitting to his status in the medical world. In 1889, Hughes became editor of the *British Homeopathic Journal*, and the British Faculty of Homeopathy still awards an annual prize that bears his name.

His authority was also recognised in America. As early as 1876 he was appointed as the permanent Secretary of the Organization of the International Congress of Homeopathy Physicians in Philadelphia, and the University of Pennsylvania conferred upon him an Honorary MD degree.

Richard Hughes became a minister at Brighton's Catholic Apostolic Church on Carlton Hill, and on his retirement went to live in the Surrey village of Albury, where Edward Irving, founder of the Catholic Apostolic movement in the 1830s, had gone to live himself. He died in Dublin in 1902 and is buried next to his wife in Albury.

With his skills in both orthopaedics and homeopathy, Sister Jane's early patients were in very capable and distinguished hands.

fundamental today. The 'ladies' referred to were of course volunteers, mainly Sisters from the Community of the Holy Cross as well as other charitably minded ladies in the community. The important thing is that none of them needed to be paid.

Word was spreading about the Home and by 1884 children were also accepted at 7 College Place, one block to the east of College Road, where Mrs Ellen Jenkins was in charge of the children. Ellen's name also appears earlier under The Invalid Home run by Matron Harriet Mills at 8 Sudeley Street in 1871. She is described as a 'Bible Woman'. Housing children in domestic properties was by no means unusual in the latter part of the 19th century. In the nearby Kemp Town estate, which incorporated 105 large houses in a square, crescent and two terraces, some 40 of the houses served as schools during the period.

Top to bottom: Drawings of the houses in Sudeley Place, College Road and College Place, early sites of St. John's Home from 1875, before it moved up the hill to Walpole Road in 1885. (Dugong John, www.dugongjohn.com)

21

Chapter 3

I have determined to build

An appeal for funds for the proposed new building. Note the already extensive list of patrons, and the reference to the impact of poverty on the 'mass of helpless suffering little children'.
(St. John's College)

PROPOSED NEW BUILDING
FOR
St. John's Convalescent Home for Children.
KEMP TOWN, BRIGHTON.

President:
THE RIGHT REV. THE LORD BISHOP OF CHICHESTER.

Patrons:
LORD EGMONT,
SIR THOMAS BARRETT LENNARD, Bart.,
SIR HENRY FLETCHER, Bart.,
SIR ALBERT SASSOON, Kt. C.S.I.,
LE BARON DA COSTA RICCI,
W. T. MARRIOTT, Esq., Q.C., M.P.,
GENERAL SANDHAM, R.A.,
GENERAL SHUTE, C.B.,
ALEX. J. R. STEWART, Esq., or Ates.
H. W. BURGESS, Esq.,

Patronesses:
THE MARCHIONESS OF ABERGAVENNY,
THE COUNTESS OF MALMESBURY,
THE LADY ISABELLA STEWART,
THE HON. MARY HENNIKER,
THE DOWAGER LADY FLETCHER,
LADY BARRETT LENNARD,
THE HON. MRS. HENRY LEGGE,
LADY STEWART WOOD.

Honorary Chaplain:
THE REV. C. H. MAUNSELL.

Consulting Committee:
REV. C. W. BOND,   REV. W. A. FIRTH,   S. WINTER FISHER, ESQ., M.D.,
REV. R. D. COCKING,   REV. C. H. MAUNSELL,   MAJOR MACDONALD HALL,
REV. T. OWEN S. DAVIES, AUGUSTUS L. COORE, ESQ., RICHARD HUGHES, ESQ., M.D.
Honorary Treasurer: COL. H. C. GROVE MORRIS.   Honorary Secretary: ARTHUR W. WOODS, ESQ.

AN APPEAL.

IN these days of over-population in large towns, of depression in trade and consequent want of work, poverty, and distress among the working classes of this country—in those days when our national sin of drunkenness leads to such wide-spread misery, pauperism, and crime, there is a class in the community which most of all deserves and sorely needs our pity, viz., the mass of helpless suffering little children. Whatever difficulties may beset other modes of helping others, whatever fear of pauperising and doing harm as well as good, to help a little sick and suffering

BY THE TIME we read the 9th Annual Report, written in 1883, which recounts the activities of the Home in the previous year, we find a resolve that will shape the course of the Home from then until now. Sister Jane followed her intention to build a new Home with the bold statement that of the £3,000 required, £2,000 had already been found (or pledged). She thus makes an appeal for funds 'to all who are interested in children, especially suffering ones'.

The site she chose, and purchased from William Percival Boxall of Belle Vue Hall, was an imposing one, at the top of Walpole Road, above the Royal Sussex County Hospital and just below the racecourse. At a height of 230 feet above sea level, the highest point in Brighton, it was certainly going to provide the pure sea air that she believed was so necessary to the recovery of invalid children. Although now a built-up area of Edwardian terraced housing and multiple hospital developments, in 1886 the location was a green field site with only three large Victorian villas below it.

The architects were Clayton and Black, a well-known Brighton firm, whose nearest work, a rather more fanciful design, can be seen at the French Convalescent Home on the seafront to the south-east. By the time building work began, the cost had risen, and so it was decided to build just the east half of the planned building. In her appeal for funds the indefatigable foundress wrote, 'one hundredth part of the cost to the public of supporting a sickly adult in the workhouse, if lovingly spent on ailing childhood, would save a wasted and joyless life'. The workhouse in Elm Grove, a short walk to the north from Walpole Road, opened in 1867. Its construction cost £41,000, significantly more than the funds Sister Jane was seeking to raise. The foundation stone of St. John's was laid in October 1886 and the building was completed by May 1887. The finished design was somewhat simpler, even starker, than Clayton and Black's original impression, reproduced on page 24. We can only assume that limited funds dictated practicality, hence curtailing the embellishments to window and door frames.

Sister Jane writes in the 12th Annual Report: '… it is with great thankfulness I have to relate that we have moved into the new Home (or rather that part of it already finished) in May last and although there was a slight tinge of regret on leaving the old houses where we had been located for so many years, yet the far greater advantages we had in view of the benefits of the change to our poor little sickly children, easily overcame these small regrets.' She goes on, as though to reassure anyone who doubts that their money has been wisely spent: 'One poor child, a chronic invalid, who has for years only gone outside the house in a perambulator, has already become so much stronger in this pure, bracing air…' She

1885 lease with William Boxall of Belle Vue Hall for the land in Walpole Road on which the Home was to be built. (St. John's College)

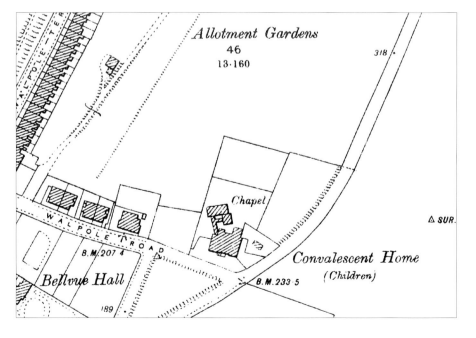

2nd edition, 1890s OS 25-inches-to-mile map showing St. John's in a relatively isolated position, with only three other villas in Walpole Road. Note the shelter in the playground, between the house and the road.

Clayton and Black's original design for the Home, which is a more embellished version of the design that was built. Note the details round doors and windows, which were to have given the Home a more countrified air. (St. John's College)

Programme for a bazaar held in the autumn of 1886. It was opened by the President of the Home, HRH Princess Mary of Teck. (St. John's College)

also reports that a 'Grand Bazaar' was inaugurated at the Corn Exchange in the centre of Brighton to help the Building Fund. It was opened by the President, HRH Princess Mary Adelaide, Duchess of Teck, and raised an impressive £505 13s 1d.

The programme for it was lavish and there was a huge range of activities spread over a three-day period. There was also a performance given by Miss Masters of her drama, *The Scarlet Dye*. This raised £82 4s 9d, a considerable sum. The play is lost; only the St. John's poster remains (see page 26).

Appended to the 14th Annual Report is an appeal, bearing the name of Colonel HC Grove Morris, for completing the building. 'Since taking possession of this finished part,' he writes, 'the want of a room for those children who temporarily fall ill so as to keep them apart from the others, or to isolate any case of illness that may require watching, has been most severely felt, as have the more prosaic needs of a coal cellar and kitchen offices.' He finishes by referring to the children's 'happy smiles' as he petitions for further contributions from the charitable.

So who were the 'charitable' who were to keep the Home going? We do not have to look far. Each Annual Report contains the names of those who had made donations or provided subscriptions, whereby convalescent beds could be 'bought' for a three-week

The first President

The first, and only, President of St. John's Home was Princess Mary Adelaide Wilhelmina Elizabeth, a granddaughter of George III and great grandmother of the present Queen. She is notable for being amongst the first members of the royal family to espouse philanthropy and actively support charities.

Born in Hanover in 1833, at the age of four she moved with her family to Kew, where she spent her childhood and young womanhood being kept largely from the public eye. For a long while her mother's earnest endeavours to find her a husband were in vain. She had little money of her own and she lacked physical grace. Her considerable girth earned her the unfortunate nickname 'Fat Mary' in the East London communities that she became accustomed to visiting. One US Ambassador estimated her weight to be 250 pounds (i.e. nearly 18 stone). How he knew this we cannot tell. Eventually, when she was 33, a dark-haired young officer in the Austrian army, Prince Francis of Teck, proposed and was accepted. On their marriage they became the Duke and Duchess of Cambridge. They had four children together, the eldest, Mary, becoming George V's Queen, although her mother did not live long enough to see their coronation.

Her married life with Francis was volatile. They were both bad with money and ran up considerable debts. As a working member of the royal family, parliament granted Princess Mary an allowance of £5,000 per annum, 20% of which she gave away to deserving charities. Queen Victoria allowed the couple an apartment in Kensington Palace, but she would not provide any further income, nor would she grant Francis royal status. Only on the occasion

HRH Princess Mary Adelaide, Duchess of Teck. Photograph by Elliott and Fry, 1888. (© National Portrait Gallery, London)

of her Golden Jubilee in 1887 did she relent somewhat and permit him to be termed 'His Highness' — but without the 'Royal' addition.

Following a period abroad, possibly evading creditors, Princess Mary became Patron of Dr Barnardo's Homes, the NSPCC and the YWCA. She also allowed her name to be connected with a number of orphanages and schools, including St. John's. She worked very hard on their behalf, helping to generate funds. In many institutions in the late Victorian era there was a great craze for bazaars, where middle class English ladies would pretend to be shopkeepers for a day or two to raise money for charities. Princess Mary at one time had six of these on the go, including the one at St. John's in 1886, which she opened.

Perhaps Princess Mary's most significant legacy is that she brought ordinary people closer to the royal family at a time when the Queen was retreating from public view during her long widowhood. She died in 1897 at the age of 63.

Advert for St. John's from an 1897 edition of the *Brighton Herald*. Princess Mary 'allowed her name to be connected with a number of orphanages and schools' and indeed full advantage was taken of this. (*Brighton Herald*)

From the list of 1884 donors. Note that ten Borradailes feature. (St. John's College)

DONATIONS AND SUBSCRIPTIONS FOR 1884.

Name	£	s.	d.
Adams, Mrs. Mayon	1	1	0
Anonymous	1	1	0
Anderson, Sir William, K.C.B.	2	2	0
A Friend	2	0	0
An old Convalescent, to help some poor child to recover health	0	10	0
Aplin, Miss C.	0	10	0
Aplin, Miss C. (don.)	0	5	0
Aplin, Miss C. (Building Fund)	1	10	0
Austen, Mrs.	1	1	0
Barnes, Messrs., & Co.	1	1	0
Bellamy, Rev. Dr.	2	2	0
Bellamy, Rev. Dr. (Building Fund)	10	0	0
Bellamy, Miss (late)	1	1	0
Benwell, Mrs.	1	1	0
Blagrave, Mrs. (don.)	5	0	0
Blaker, Mrs.	0	10	0
Borradaile, Mrs. (late)	1	0	0
Borradaile, Mrs. (Surbiton)	1	1	0
Borradaile, Mrs. John	2	2	0
Borradaile, Rev. Ernest	1	1	0
Borradaile, Mrs. Ernest	1	1	0
Borradaile, Miss E.	0	2	6
Borradaile, Miss E. A. (late)	1	1	0
Borradaile, Miss G. M.	1	1	0
Borradaile, Miss H. A.	1	1	0
Borradaile, Wee Dorathy B.	0	5	0
Bowen, James, Esq.	1	1	0
Bowen, Miss Hilda M. (Collecting Box)	0	18	0
Brankstone, Mrs.	0	10	0
Bridge, Miss Fanny M.	1	1	0
Bridport, Viscountess	1	1	0
Brown, Miss	1	1	0
Burges, William, Esq. (1st don.)	1	0	0
Burges, William, Esq. (2nd don.)	1	0	0
Burges, Mrs. (1st don.)	1	0	0
Burges, Mrs. (2nd don.)	1	1	0
Burges, Miss (Collecting Card)	0	12	0
Burges, Miss (Collecting Card)	0	15	0
Busk, Mrs. Charles	1	1	0
Busk, Mrs. John	1	1	0
E. and R.	0	4	0
Clark, Mrs.	2	2	0
Clayton, Miss	0	5	0
Cole, Rev. T. H.	0	10	0
Courtney, Mrs.	0	10	0
Currey, Edmund Charles, Esq.	0	10	6
Currey, Miss	0	2	6
Davis, Mr.	0	5	0
Edmonds, Mr. (don.)	0	2	6
Edwards, Mrs.	0	5	0
Ellis, Mrs. (Collecting Card, Building Fund)	1	7	0
Ellis, Mrs. Stephenson	0	10	6
Ellis, Miss (Blackheath)	1	1	0
Ellis, Miss (Clapham)	2	2	0
Evans, Mrs. David	1	1	0
F. E. M. H.	5	0	0
Finney, J. D., Esq.	1	1	0
Forbes, Miss M. Douglas	1	1	0
Forster, Mrs. (don.)	5	0	0
Fryer, Miss	1	1	0
Giles, Mrs. Galley	0	10	6
Godsell, Edmund, Esq.	0	10	0
Goodrich, Mrs.	0	10	0
Goodrich, Mrs. (don.)	0	10	0
Goldsmith, Mrs. (late)	0	10	0
Goldsmith, Miss	1	0	0
Green, Miss (Building Fund)	10	0	0
Greville-Nugent, The Hon Mrs.	1	0	0
Grueber, Thomas, Esq. (Building Fund)	1	1	0
Hannington, Messrs., and Sons	1	1	0
Harmar, Mrs. (late)	1	1	0
Harmar, Mrs. Ambrose	4	4	0
Harmar, George, Esq.	1	1	0
Harris, Miss F.	1	1	0
Hawthorne, Miss E. J.	1	1	0
Headlam, Miss	0	2	6
Heale, Mrs.	1	1	0
Hedley, Miss I.	1	1	0
Hedley, Miss I. (Building Fund)	25	0	0
Herapath, Mrs.	1	1	0
Hills, Rev, William Jeffreys	1	1	0
Hodge, Miss M. E.	1	1	0
Hodge, Miss P. L. (don.)	1	0	0
Holmes, Mrs.	1	1	0
Hopkins, Mrs. Manly	0	10	0
Humphreys, Mrs.	1	1	0
Hunt, Mrs.	1	1	0
Hunter, Mrs.	0	10	0
Jones, Mrs. Meyrick	0	10	0
Kayess, Miss L. (Collecting Card)			
Latham, Mrs.	2	5	6
Lawrence, John, Esq.	1	1	0
Legg, Mrs.	1	1	0
Lloyd, Miss (Ewell)	1	0	0
Lloyd, Miss (Ewell)			
Lloyd, Mrs. (late, London)	1	1	0
Lloyd, Mrs. (late, Building Fund)	2	2	0
Lloyd, Miss (London)	3	0	0
Lloyd, Miss (London, Building Fund)	2	2	0
Lloyd, Miss Jessie (London)	2	0	0
Longman & Co., Messrs.	2	0	0
Maberly, Miss	1	1	0
Maugles, Miss	0	5	0
Maunsell, Rev. C. H.	5	0	0
Maunsell, Rev. C. H. (Building Fund)	5	0	0
Metz, Mrs. Von (Collecting Card)	1	5	6
Moberly, W. H., Esq.	2	2	0
Moore, Mrs.	1	1	0
Morgan, Mrs.	1	1	0
Morley, Miss	1	1	0
Murray, Mrs.	1	1	0
Offertory (St. James' Church, Waltham)	1	1	10
Owen, Mrs. (don.)	2	0	0
Paine, Cornelius, Esq.	1	1	0
Paine, Mrs.	0	10	6
Paine, Mrs.	0	10	0
Paine, Mrs. Hammon	3	0	0
Paine, Miss Hammon	0	10	0
Parker, Herbert, Esq.	5	0	0
Penn, Mrs.			
Prendergast, Miss A.			
Pullan, Mrs.			
Pulien, Mrs.			
Punch, Mrs.			
Punch, Mrs. (Building Fund)			
Pullyn, Miss K. (Building Fund)			
Ramsey, Mrs.			
Rasch, Miss			
Reid, G. Lowe, Esq.			
Rucker, Mrs.			
Sandeman, Mrs.			
Sandham, Rev. J. M.			
Sandham, General R. A.			
Saunders, Francis R., Esq.			
Savory, Mrs.			
Senior, Mrs.			
Senior, Mrs. (Building Fund)			
Sheffield, Miss C. (Building Fund)			
Shuckburg, Mrs.			
Shuldham, Miss Maria H. S.			
Shuldham, Miss Maria H. S. (Building Fund)			
Sibthorp, Miss			
Smith, Mrs. Charles			
Smith, Mrs. James (don.)			
Soames, Mrs. J. K.			
Stigant, Miss			
Storrar, Miss			
Street, H., Esq.			
Street, H. W., Esq.			
Swinburn, Joseph, Esq.			
Thornton, Rev. C. G.			
Trollope, Miss			
Tylden, Mrs.			
Verrall, Mrs. Jenner			
Visconti, Countess			
Wagner, Rev. A. D.			
Wallace, Mrs.			
Webb, Mrs.			
Whatley, A. J., Esq.			
White, Fred A., Esq.			
White, The Misses (the late, Brighton)			
White, Miss (Blackheath)			
Willett, G. W., Esq.			
Wilson, James, Esq.			
Wilson, Miss			
Windrus, Miss G. E.			
Wood, Miss, Lady Superintendent of the Children's Hospital, Great Ormond St.			
Wright, Stephen, Esq.			

The Misses S. & E. Borradaile, a free Cot in the Home ..
Miss Dampier retains a Cot in the Home ..
Miss Richards retains a Cot in the Home ..
By sale of Waste Paper (per Miss H. A. Borradaile) ..

Poster for *The Scarlet Dye*. This drama by Miss Julia Masters is now lost; only the poster remains. Miss Borradaile wrote in her report: 'I am much indebted to [Miss Masters] and her friends for their kind exertions, the good result of which was £82 4s 9d, which sum Miss Masters handed over to the Building Fund.' (St. John's College)

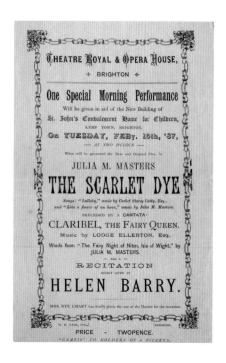

THEATRE ROYAL & OPERA HOUSE, BRIGHTON

One Special Morning Performance

Will be given in aid of the New Building of St. John's Convalescent Home for Children, KEMP TOWN, BRIGHTON,

On TUESDAY, FEBy. 15th, '87,
AT TWO O'CLOCK.

When will be presented the New and Original Play, by

JULIA M. MASTERS

THE SCARLET DYE

Songs: "Lullaby," music by Corbet Stacey Catty, Esq.
and "Like a flower of an hour," music by Julia M. Masters.

PRECEDED BY A CANTATA

CLARIBEL, THE FAIRY QUEEN.

Music by LODGE ELLERTON, Esq.
Words from "The Fairy Night of Niton, Isle of Wight," by JULIA M. MASTERS.

AND A

RECITATION

KINDLY GIVEN BY

HELEN BARRY.

MRS. NYE CHART has kindly given the use of the Theatre for the occasion.

PRICE - TWOPENCE.
GRATIS TO HOLDERS OF TICKETS.

period for the cost of one guinea (i.e. 105 pence). The names of some 280 donors and subscribers are listed for the year from 1 July 1888. Among them were ten Borradailes, assuring us that there was plenty of family support for the venture. Clear instructions were given as to where and when cheques were to be paid. Post Office Orders were to be made out to Miss Jane Borradaile at The Post Office, College Road – the building currently occupied by Brighton College Bursary.

In 1890, once the first part of the Home was complete and being used to good effect, the foundations were laid for the chapel, a building that was to remain the focus of the children's daily lives. The West Wing was also built and the playground was levelled, which made a huge difference to the children. In the Annual Report for 1890 it was announced that 'in order to place the Home on a more substantial basis and to relieve Miss Borradaile of her great responsibility, a committee has been appointed and Col HC Grove Morris has kindly consented to act as Chairman'.

An indenture of 17 December 1889 marks the official start of St. John's Convalescent Home as a charitable trust. The triple purpose of the Home was confirmed as 1) a temporary home for convalescent children; 2) a permanent home for crippled children; and 3) a school for training girls as domestic servants. The indenture goes on in the characteristic language of the law:

Christ's Little Citizens

Chapel life for residents of St. John's

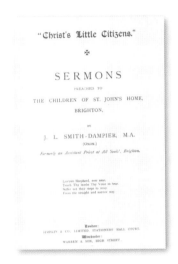

Frontispiece of *Christ's Little Citizens*, sermons for children by JL Smith Dampier, 1902. (Royal Pavilion and Museums, Brighton and Hove)

In 1889, just three years after the School had moved into the Walpole Road premises, Sister Jane decided that she must have a chapel, which duly happened. It opened in 1890 and the children went there daily (twice on Sundays), with confession on Fridays.

We know from Gwen Hanks' account of her time there (see page 38) that when attending chapel, children in the east wing wore blue caps and those in the west wing wore pink, and they sat on opposite sides, even entering the chapel through different doors.

The Home was in the parish of All Souls in Eastern Road (demolished in 1968 for road widening) and the vicar would regularly take services until a chaplain was appointed. The curate of All Souls, the Rev JL Smith Dampier, published a book of sermons in 1902 entitled *Christ's Little Citizens*, which he dedicated to the children of the Home, of whom he was clearly fond. There is much well-meant advice in his well-crafted addresses; for instance on Low Sunday 1901, 'You must try to please HIM at school by working at your lessons as well as you possibly can.' Then on 17 June, speaking about love: 'It must be far-reaching and unselfish, as St Martin gave his cloak to a beggar... Be kind to animals too.' And on 3 August: 'Through baptism we are all adopted into God's family.' (He was a kindly man, aware of the less than happy backgrounds that many of his young congregation came from.) Later,

there was a patriotic theme: 'As the Union Jack is the banner of the English army, the cross is the banner of Christ's army. Fight under Christ's banner.' He expected the reader to be patient, however. On 3 February 1901 his sermon about vineyards ran to eight pages.

The chapel remained at the centre of life at St. John's after it became a school. In November 1957, the Headmaster asked that members of the Board should attend Sunday chapel individually 'as a source of great encouragement to the children'. Dennis Forster appointed the last chaplain in 1987. In due course the chapel was put to other uses; firstly it became a common room, and it has now been converted into a space for the production of music and drama.

The chapel as it is now, converted into a performance space, with a lighting rig and walls covered by curtains. (Ian Muir Photographer)

Laying of the foundation stone for the chapel in 1890. An impressive procession of clergy, nuns and children is shown to be in attendance. (St. John's College)

St. John's chapel, with its striking Victorian wall paintings, in the 1890s, the first decade of its existence. Billie writes (see page 42) 'They would usher us into an awe-inspiring church... The place was very hallowed and hushed, and smelt of polish.' (St. John's College)

'At the present time the Charity is under the sole superintendence and control of the donor, subject to whose superintendence and control its various branches are carried on and conducted as regards working details by herself assisted by non resident and resident lady volunteers.' In short, Sister Jane would continue to be in charge. A condition of the charity was that each of its Trustees should be a member of the Church of England '...and if any of the trustees ceases to be a member of the Church of England...he shall thereupon become incapable of acting in the trust'. We remember that Jane was an Associate Sister of an Anglican Community and that the Church played a central role in the life of the Home. The front of all official documents contained the line, beneath the heading: 'Under the Sanction of the Right Rev the Lord Bishop of Chichester'. Prime position was also accorded to HRH Princess Mary Adelaide, Duchess of Cambridge, who was to serve as President until her death in 1897.

Chapter 4

A bright, happy little family

The chronic ward in the early 1900s. Set up in 1904, it was here that the most serious cases committed to Sister Jane's care came. It was threatened with closure in 1920, but funds issuing from an appeal were sufficient to keep it open. (St. John's College)

THE HOME MUST have resembled a huge building site for the first five or so years of its existence, but its function as a convalescent home continued unabated. In her 1892 Report Sister Jane writes, almost proudly, that one poor sickly little child has been cured and sent home to her parents. Two years later she says 'it is cheering to watch the improvement made by poor London children'. By 1902, she was able to report

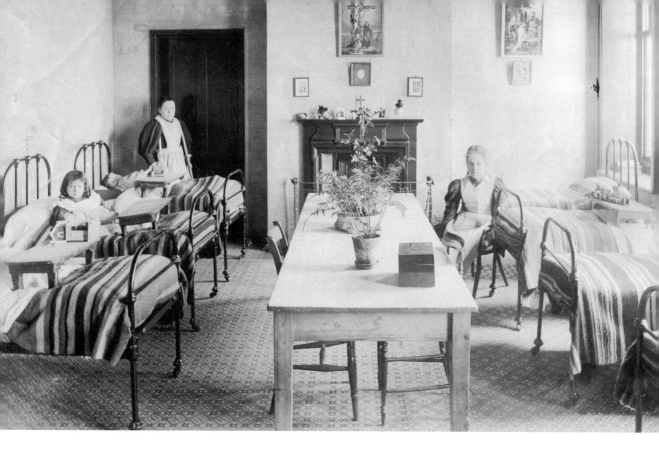

The chronic ward. Note the religious imagery on the fireplace wall. (St. John's College)

that 380 convalescent children had been taken into the Home during the previous year. She refers to the more permanent residents as being 'a bright, happy little family party having their own lady attendants'. Like children in any other family they become victims of childhood infections; thus in the spring of 1903 the Home was closed following an outbreak of measles. That year, 352 convalescents were received. In 1904 an indication is given of the way the Home was expanding: there were 16 girls, aged from 14 to 17, training for domestic service, 12 Home (or long-stay) children, eight cots in the newly opened chronic ward and seven crippled girls in the needlework party.

By 1905, the Home children no longer had to attend the National School because a schoolroom had been arranged. It would be another 23 years before the Home was recognised as a 'Home School of Recovery'.

The children in the chronic ward were a continuing concern. 'Eddie and Alfie are taken for drives in summer, compelled to lie in the carriages' and 'Miss E Borradaile took the helpless cripples to St Anne's Well [gardens in Hove] and laid them under trees on benches'. Later, 'A girl of 14 is still on her back but growing. She is busy with needlework.' The Home was aware of the difficulties faced by parents: 'Many of our little guests are very poor. Mothers evidently find it a hard matter to send them properly equipped, some coming with scarcely enough clothing for one week.' Always there was a sense of optimism about the benefits of their stay: 'The poor sad little faces on arrival [are] so changed into bright rosy cheeks it is difficult to believe.' Not all of the sojourns of the 'little guests' at St. John's ended happily. In the Report for 1916, which the war necessitated being short, we read: 'One dear little girl Beatrice has been taken to rest after much suffering.'

The Schoolroom. The children's concentration on their various tasks is not so very different from what we might expect today. However, the smocks and uniform haircuts speak of a different age. (St. John's College)

During the war Jane Borradaile herself was weakening, and on 12 January 1918 she died. A Requiem Mass was sung for her five days later at All Souls, Eastern Road. The notice in the *Brighton Evening Argus* reports that the coffin had rested in the chapel at the Home all the previous evening, watched over by four Sisters of Mercy of the Home. There followed a service at the borough cemetery,[7] where 'the mourners gathered round the grave and the remains of a faithful servant were committed to the earth. The floral tributes were exquisite and numerous.'

7   Now Woodvale Crematorium and Cemetery.

Nuns in the sitting room; Sister Jane is on the left. Note the precarious pipework for the gas lighting. (St. John's College)

31

Chapter 5

Under the management of the Community

IN HER WILL Sister Jane bequeathed over £500 to the Home. In the 1919 Annual Report, the committee reassured friends of St. John's that the Home would continue as before:

> Since last year's Report was issued, St. John's Home has been passing through a period of change. At the request of the Foundress, the Sisters of the Holy Cross agreed many years ago to undertake the care of the Home at her resignation or death. The promise has been fulfilled, and five Sisters are now working in it and are in charge of the various departments, assisted by some ladies who helped Sister Jane Borradaile. The work continues on the same lines and in the same spirit of devotion to the cause of the sick and ailing children.

A change of management meant modernisation of the fabric of the building. The place was done up, which necessitated expenditure, and money was spent that was not there. Stocks were sold and debt ensued. By 1920, the chronic ward was threatened with closure. In September an appeal appeared in the *Brighton and Hove Parochial Gazetteer*, which read:

> How many possibilities St. John's has, and how impossible it is to fill them. The structure is most solidly built, its position is ideal, there are two playgrounds with shelters and two large kitchen gardens, but the Home has no endowment and is supported only by voluntary contributions. The demand for

beds is increasing, as it is recognized that sea air, and especially Brighton sea air, is the thing that is needed for cases of nerve shock and tuberculosis. At the time of writing the Home has fifty more and keep them filled, but these we must dream about, for, sad to say, the ward containing 22 of the present beds (those for the more invalid children) will shortly have to be closed if help does not come from somewhere. £1,000 is needed to clear off the debt and set the Home on a firm basis.

Sister Cecilia, who took over as Sister Superior after Sister Jane's death, was succeeded by Sister Helena Mary and all the evidence is that funds were forthcoming to keep the chronic ward open. Furthermore, new treatments were being carried out in the post-war period as is evidenced by the 1921 Annual Report: 'Many little patients have benefited from electrical treatment and massage and remedial therapy given by the Hon Clarice Rendell and other ladies.' This electrical therapy sounds an alarming course of action. In fact, the device used would have been popular in the late Victorian/Edwardian era almost as a form of parlour entertainment. A group of willing participants would stand in a circle holding hands, two of them holding a terminal of a device that emitted a low voltage current. The ensuing series of mild electric shocks was believed to sharpen reactions and enliven the spirits.

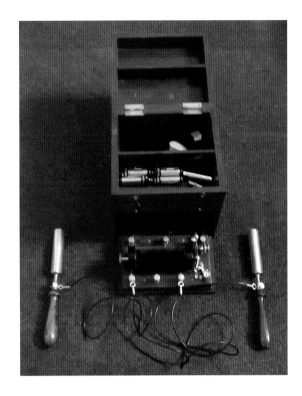

The electric shock machine used to enliven the spirits of the little patients. Today electroconvulsive treatment is still used to support individuals who display a range of mental disorders. (With thanks to Oliver Smyth)

The 1923 Annual Report laments that mumps kept children in isolation at a time of many applications. An open-air ward for 12 girls was opened in the playground, which proved successful and was to continue for some years. The Home also made a modest profit of £44 after the previous two years' debts of £956 and £427.

The year 1923 was the first one in which the Annual Report was specific about the diseases afflicting the children. The list of over 90 conditions from which children were recovering reads like the index in a medical directory, with its almost Victorian preoccupation with categories and sub-categories. 'General Debility' was then and would continue to be the principal reason for children being there. This 'General Debility' was the consequence of the poor air, inadequate diet, and unhealthy living conditions that caused Sister Jane to set up the Home nearly 50 years earlier.

That landmark was celebrated in 1925, the Home's Jubilee Year. There was much to celebrate since the Home had first started in the modest surroundings of 9 Sudeley Place in 1875. A ball was held at Sherry's in May, and in the same month a tea party was held there for the children, when a 'gramaphone [sic]' was presented to them.

There were 299 admissions that year. The success of the open-air ward was again referred to and the surplus for the year was £136. The list of subscribers and donors runs to 13 pages on the 30-page report, but funds were 'still urgently needed' as a request to this effect in emboldened type at the end of the report reminds us. The cost per patient in 1926 was £1 2s 10d, compared with 19s 10d the previous year. These were difficult financial times nationally and the Home was not immune to the escalation of costs that everyone else was experiencing.

On 4 June 1928, Hilda Maud Lindo became the School's first Headmistress. This was a pivotal moment for St. John's in that for the first time teaching in a school (as

17

LIST OF DISEASES AND OPERATIONS from which Patients were certified to be convalescent on entry.

Disease		Disease	
Adenitis, Cervical	5	Nervous Debility	5
Adenitis, Inguinal	1	Neuritis	1
Adenoids	1	Otitis Media	4
Anaemia	33	Paralysis, Functional	1
Asthma	2	Paralysis, Infantile	1
Backward Development	2	Paralysis, Spastic	1
Blood Poisoning	1	Paraplegia, Infantile Spastic	1
Boils	2	Phlebitis	1
Bronchiestasis	2	Phthisis	2
Bronchitis, Acute	13	Pleurisy	2
Bronchitis, Chronic	2	Pneumonia	5
Catarrh, Bronchial	9	Pneumonia, Broncho	5
Catarrh, Gastric	1	Pyaemia	1
Catarrh, Nasal	2	Rheumatism	4
Chorea	8	Rheumatoid Arthritis	1
Concussion	2	Shock	1
Conjunctivitis	2	Spinal Curvature	1
Constipation, Chronic	1	Synovitis	1
Coxa Vara	1	Thyroid, Enlarged	1
Cystitis	1	Tonsillitis	10
Dyspepsia	2	TUBERCULOUS DISEASE :—	
Emphysema	1	Glands of Neck	3
Encephalitis	1	Lungs, Quiescent	1
Fracture, Forearm	1	Sinus of Scapula	1
General Debility	38	Spinal, Arrested	1
Goitre, Exophthalmic	1	Typhoid Fever	1
Glands, Enlarged Bronchial	1	Venereal Disease	2
HEART, Diseases of	16	Whooping Cough	1
Cardiac Weakness	4	Wound of Thigh	1
Congenital Disease	1	OPERATIONS :—	
Dilated Heart	3	Abscess Abdominal Wall	1
D. A. H.	1	Amputation of Breast	2
Heart Failure, slight	1	Appendicitis	8
Irregular Heart	3	Deformity of Foot	1
Mitral Disease	2	Gastric Ulcer	1
Myocarditis	1	Gastro-Enterostomy	1
Haemorrhage (Puberty)	1	Hernia, Femoral Strangulated	1
Hysteria	1	Inguinal Abscess	1
Impetigo	2	Phimosis	1
Influenza	2	Mastitis	1
Keratitis, Interstitial	1	Mastoid	5
Malnutrition	3	Multiple Fibroids Uteri	1
Marasmus	1	Tonsils and Adenoids	7
Measles, and complications of	2	Tonsillectomy	1
Mumps	1	Varicose Veins	1
Nephritis	3		

The 1923 Annual Report. The list of diseases from which children came to convalesce appeared for the first time in this report. The practice continued until 1956. (St. John's College)

Sherry's

Sherry's Dance Hall opened in Brighton's West Street in 1919. Previous buildings on the site, which extends back into Middle Street, were variously the home of Mr and Mrs Henry Thrale, who famously entertained Dr Johnson in the late 18th century, a concert hall, a roller-skating rink, and a 2,000-seat cinema.

Sherry's features prominently in Graham Greene's *Brighton Rock* (1938): "'Let's go to Sherry's," Pinkie said, "I hate the place.'" Whatever Pinkie perversely thought of it, it was an immensely popular venue in Brighton in the years between the wars, not only for dancing, but also for private parties and children's events. Thus we see that in May 1923 a St. John's fund-raising ball was held there, and in the same month there was a party for the children there.

Pinkie's world of crime and evil is a far cry from St Helena Mary's Home in Walpole Road, but she would have known as well as anyone that fund-raising is best conducted in the most popular venues.

Sherry's advert from the *Brighter Brighton Guide* (May 1923). An unnamed source reports that Sherry's was a regular haunt of St. John's staff on Friday evenings well into the 1970s. The staff now congregate in the Round Georges in Sutherland Road. (*Brighter Brighton Guide*)

Sherry's in West Street. This building, which stretches between West Street and Middle Street, has seen a number of uses; it has been, amongst other things, a concert hall, an ice rink and (as we see in the photograph) a bingo hall. It is now a night club. (With thanks to the Regency Society)

CHILDREN'S TEA AT SHERRY'S.

On May 10th, thanks to the generosity of Sherry's, a tea was able to be given to the children of St. John's Convalescent Home. They had a most enjoyable afternoon with balloons and caps galore, in carnival style. Among the company present were Lady Forwood, the Hon. Mr. and Mrs. de Trafford, who supplied the sweets, Councillor Michael Marten, Mr. and Mrs Solly Goodman, who supplied the Char-a-banc and the oranges, Mr. and Mrs. Hughes, Mr. and Mrs. Scutt, Mrs. Cartwright, Mrs. Morrison, Mr. David, Mrs. Edith Venus, Miss Borradaile, Miss Charlton, Mrs. Mabel Smith. Before their departure the children gave three cheers for those who had entertained them, and also for Sherry's management. We congratulate Mrs. Hughes as organiser on her energetic work for the children's pleasure. During the afternoon a magnificent gramaphone was presented by the Committee to the Convalescent Home.

Children's tea party press cutting from 1923 *Brighter Brighton Guide*. Note the unusual spelling of 'gramaphone', presumably a short-lived spelling for a device that was still relatively new. (*Brighter Brighton Guide*)

distinct from care in a home) was being given an emphasis. For the next 22 years Hilda Lindo would set the tone to be that of a school.

In 1928 recognition came from the Board of Education. It was reported:

> As most children require prolonged convalescence to restore them to health and strength, for some years education according to their needs has been given, and the great event of the past year is the recognition by the Board of Education given to this side of the work, and St. John's is now certified as a Home School of Recovery.

This was official recognition of what St. John's had been doing for some time, and it meant that it could now be referred to as a school, not just as a home.

Training for domestic service

The third function of Sister Jane's Home, after caring for convalescent and crippled children, was the training of orphan girls for domestic service. We learn something of this life from Gwen Hanks' account of her time there in the 30s (see page 38). Gwen would have entered a working world where domestic service was less of a career option than it had been in the middle of the previous century. In the 1851 census over 550,000 people, predominantly women, were in domestic service and this figure did not alter much until after the First World War.

For example, the 1901 census shows that in Brighton's Lewes Crescent, just a short distance from St. John's, there was an abundance of servants. No 1, Fife House, was the home of the Duke and Duchess of Fife and their two young daughters. They had 16 servants, five men and 11 women, ranging from the Private Secretary to the Duke, through the butler, cook and housekeeper, to the nursery maids and kitchen maids. This is the sort of household that has been glamourised for television

Mrs Isabella Beeton by Maull & Polybank. Hand-tinted albumen print, 1857. (© National Portrait Gallery, London)

audiences since the servantless era of the 1970s and 80s. More modestly, up the road at No 7 a family of five had three servants to look after them – a cook, a parlour maid and a kitchen maid – which was more the norm for an upper middle class family.

Mrs Isabella Beeton in her 1861 *Book of Household Management*, which sold over 60,000 copies in its first year of publication, has an extensive section on the training and care of servants. She leaves her reader with no illusions about the plight of many, or most, of the girls who entered service:

The general servant or maid-of-all-work is perhaps the only one of her class deserving of our commiseration: her life is a solitary one and, in some places, her work is never done. She is also subject to rougher treatment than either the house or kitchen maid. She starts in life, probably a girl of 13, with some small tradesman's wife as mistress just a step or two above

By the 1927 Annual Report, 421 convalescents had passed through the Home during the previous year as well as six training girls. This is the last reference to the domestic training that was part of the Home's purpose. We can only assume that at some point soon after this date such training was phased out altogether as the demand for maidservants was severely reduced in the post-First World War era. Domestic advances (hot and cold running water and washing machines) were beginning to make household chores less onerous for the housewife, and there were so many more job opportunities open to women after they had forged their way into the workforce during the war. Sister Helena realised there was no point in training girls when there were fewer and fewer positions to be found for them. However, we know that girls were still being trained for domestic service in 1930 because of the recollection of Gwen Hanks in August 1991:

her in the social scale, and although the class contains some excellent, kind, good-hearted women, it also contains some very rough specimens of the feminine gender…

We must hope that Sister Jane and whichever sister had charge of training the girls did not allow them to enter a position with such a 'rough specimen' as a mistress. We do know that life in the Home was arduous and highly regulated, but cheerful. Nevertheless, serving the sisters and the convalescent and disabled children at table was likely to have been more companionable than the inevitably lonely existence in some households.

Domestic trainees with Sister Caroline. (Community of the Holy Cross, Costock)

I went to St. John's Convalescent Home for children, on October 7th 1930, at the age of 14. I was born on Aug 22 1916. My reason was to be trained in all things domestic, with a view to progressing to looking after the children there and finally becoming a trained Nursery Nurse, after further training, at the age of 17½, at the Hove Day Nursery, with babies up to 5 years. At S.J.H., they catered for 84 children – aged 5–15 years – who mainly came through the Invalid Children's Aid Association in London. They stayed for a few weeks – to a few months – or even years, greatly benefiting from the care, nursing, good food and sea air. Sister Helena Mary of Holy Cross was the Sr Superior, with seven sisters from the Holy Cross Convent at Haywards Heath – all playing their part in the smooth running of the Home. Sister Caroline was in charge of the 'training girls' – with the help of Miss Carmen the Matron. I remember also Sr Sophia, Sr Kate, Sr Erminilde, Sr Audrey and Sr Katherine, with Sr Salome – in a grey habit – as opposed to all the others in black.

The children were divided into the East Wing, West Wing and 'top nursery' – the youngest group of about 12 children. There were teachers for lessons – a Miss Lindo and Miss Butler – and these were often on the Balcony in good weather – which overlooked the houses to the Royal Sussex County Hospital, leading down the steep hill to the sea. Adjoining Sr Helena Mary's office was the Secretary's office, where Miss Pratt and one other lady kept all the paperwork in order. There were large gardens surrounding the Home – where most of the vegetables were grown, and a large playground and shelters for the children and other garden areas for the staff to use.

We had a beautiful chapel, which we attended regularly, including Confessions on Fridays. A Father Hrouda or Father Tyler officiated. The East Wing children wore blue chapel caps and sat on one side of the aisle and the West Wing had pink. Nurse Hilda Holt was in charge of the East Wing children and Nurse Dorothy Porter was in the West Wing. Nurse Helen Hunt took charge of the nursery. There was a large kitchen in the basement – presided over by Miss Birch and helped by Sister Mary Clare – who went into the Religious Life at Holy Cross after leaving S.J.H – and only died in 1989 at Rempstone. I well remember the kitchen, with its large black kitchen range and tiled floor – we all had to take a turn at cleaning and polishing – and the tiles were washed in hot water to which paraffin had been added! The food was plain but wholesome, and was hauled up to the children's dining rooms on the first floor by a rope-operated wooden lift. All the girls had their various duties to perform – bed making, cleaning of dormitories and staff rooms and sister's rooms etc., and a turn at vegetable preparation and learning to wait at the staff dining table. All in all we had an excellent training – and I remember Sister Kate having the task of coming along and wiping her fingers along a ledge – and deciding if it had to be cleaned again! Sister Audrey was very deaf – but managed to take us for Singing and Drama once a week, with a Madam Johnson as pianist – and on occasions, we went to entertain in private homes! Sister Katherine used to be in charge for sewing and mending once a week, in the evening. We had a free hour in the evening but it was bed at 8.30pm – ready for a 6.30am 'start' to our day.

We were invited to visit the Convent at Hayward's Heath on the feast of Corpus Christi – and we looked forward to this. After the service in the

Sister Caroline. Gwen Hanks remembers her being in charge of the 'training girls' in 1930. (Community of the Holy Cross, Costock)

Magnus Volk, inventor

The clock tower at the junction of North Street and Queen's Road is one of Brighton's most conspicuous landmarks. Dismissively described by Pevsner as 'worthless', it was erected in 1888 to mark Queen Victoria's Golden Jubilee. It is surmounted by a golden ball, which rises and falls on the hour. This quirky feature, only rarely in full working order, was designed by the local inventor Magnus Volk. The son of an immigrant German clockmaker, Volk was born at 40 Western Road, and spent most of his life in Brighton. He established the first telephone link (to a friend's house) in Brighton, fitted his own house with electric light in 1880, and did the same for the Royal Pavilion and the Corn Exchange complex. He also invented a fire alarm linked to the fire station.

His most enduring legacy was Britain's first electric railway, which opened in 1883. A car with mahogany sides and blue velvet curtains was built to run along a line for 300 yards between the Aquarium and the Chain Pier. Despite setbacks caused by storm damage and even sabotage from cab drivers and others who saw their livelihood threatened by the attraction, it proved popular and the line was extended to Black Rock in 1937. In the summer of 1940, when the beaches were closed, the railway was shut down and both terminals demolished. Following these fallow war years the line was re-opened in 1948 with seven restored cars. It was closed again in 2016 and re-opened in the summer of 2018 with new terminal buildings and an information centre.

The life of an inventor can be a precarious one. In 1887 Volk was declared bankrupt. He rented out his house in King's Road and moved to the less expensive Queen's Park Road. The following year he built an electric car for Sultan Abdul Hamid of Turkey and also persuaded him to buy an electric launch. In 1903 he moved to a farm in Hassocks before finally retiring to 128 Dyke Road in 1914, where today there is a plaque commemorating him.

Magnus Volk was a colourful character whose inventive nature was sure to appeal to the children at St. John's. There are two references to him in the annual reports. The first was in 1904, where we read: 'Mr Volk gave the children a treat at his farm in Hassocks.' Then in 1937, the year of his death, Mr Volk is thanked for 'giving the children free rides on his electric railway'. He was an entertaining and gregarious character to the very end!

Inset: Magnus Volk (1851–1937). Here he is seen in 1937 riding in the front of the train, with his right hand raised, perhaps operating the whistle. The driver seems somewhat over-dressed for his role! (Royal Pavilion and Museum, Brighton and Hove)

An early view of Volk's Electric Railway in the 1880s. (With thanks to the Regency Society)

The Haywards Heath House, shortly after the building of the chapel in the 1930s. (Community of the Holy Cross, Costock)

lovely chapel — we followed in the procession behind the Monstrance and canopy — and all the sisters — on a rhododendron-strewn pathway — into the wood, where there was a Calvary — and it always seemed to fall on a beautiful sunny day. It left an indelible memory for me.

After 3 years, I left S.J.H. and went to the Hove Day Nursery where I completed my nursery training and passed my exams and became a fully qualified Nursery Nurse. My first post was with 2 children in Hove — and when I left there I returned to St. John's as a Staff Nurse in the 'top nursery' (I'd missed the companionship of all the girls). After a year, I went into a private family — who was the sister of the then Matron — and finally moved on to become Nanny to Field Marshal Montgomery's two [nephews].

I look back on all those formative years with much love and gratitude. Sister Caroline always kept in touch — I still have her letters — and then Sister Mary Clare and Sister Mary Laurence have kindly kept in touch and I look forward to the annual newsletter every year. During my training at the Day Nursery, I could always go back 'home' to S.J.H on my free weekends, and always looked at it as 'home'.

The last news I had of the Home is that it was a Boarding School for Backward boys.

Our training and 'keep' were free, and we had 2/– (40p) per month for spending money. What a contrast to today — but happy, happy days!

This remarkably lucid and candid account of life at the Home in 1930 contributes much to our understanding of how it operated. The omnipresence of the Sisters and the centrality of the chapel (in which pink or blue caps were worn) is marked; but so too is the hard work that the girls were obliged to undertake as part of their training. Above all, Gwen was happy there and had much genuine affection for the Sisters, which was evidently reciprocated by them.

The 1937 Annual Report records that in the previous year Mr Volk (see page 39) had given the children rides on his electric railway. There was also a note of thanks to the girls of Bromley High School for toys and books 'enabling parcels to be made up on Christmas Day for those children who received no presents from their own homes'. Along with Brighton and Hove High School and St Mary's Hall in Brighton, this was a school that year after year made St. John's its charity. The year 1937 also saw the Coronation of King George V and Queen Mary, whose own mother had been the Home's first President (see page 25). All of the children were presented with a Coronation mug, donated by the Brighton Committee.

Chapter 6

Waifs and Strays and war again

BY 1937, SISTER Helena Mary's health was failing and she decided after 17 years in the post to retire from her position as Sister Superior. The Sisters of the Holy Cross resolved that the best way forward would be to hand over responsibility for the Home to another religious community. In a letter to the Secretary of the Invalid Children's Aid Association on 28 July 1937, Sister Helena Mary writes:

> The Community of the Holy Cross have very regretfully come to the decision to give up St. John's Home. We should have liked another religious community to have carried on the work, but so far we have been quite unsuccessful, and for the same reason we are giving up – inability to spare the sisters… The income is about £6000. It is for 84 children, and is certified by the Board of Education. Is there any hope that the ICAA would consider taking it over?

On 12 August the committee of ICAA decided 'with very great regret that they could not accept this offer'. A similar letter on 13 August was more successful and eventually it came under the auspices of The Waifs and Strays Society (see page 43). In the meantime, the Home still had to be run following Sister Helena Mary's departure. The minutes of a meeting of the Trustees on 23 August 1937 state that the following resolution was passed:

> 1) Miss Green to be asked to be Superintendent of the Home from the withdrawal of the Sisters on 1st December 1937 until the Home is taken over by another institution on the following terms. Salary £156 per annum together with board and lodging for herself and her mother. Bonus of £50 to be offered her in compensation for any financial loss owing to the uncertainty of the permanence of the appointment. 3 months notice on either side.

> 2) Miss Green to have as an assistant a Nursing Matron who must be a State Registered Nurse and a house matron and junior clerk in addition to the existing secular staff.

3) The trusteeship and management of the Home to be offered to the Church of England Waifs and Strays Society.

A letter from the Board of Education in November 1937 agrees to the appointment of Miss Isabel Green as Matron. This is after expressing 'its appreciation of the valuable work that has been done by the Home under its present management in the cause of the delicate child'.

By mid-November official confirmation came from St. John's solicitor, C Villiers Johnson, that The Waifs and Strays 'had now definitely decided to take it over'. This involved nominating '7 Gentlemen to be trustees in the place of the trustees who are retiring'. Thus began an arrangement that was to remain in place for the next 20 years.

One of Miss Green's early patients would have been William (Billie) Godfrey from Hackney in East London. He, like so many other children, was excited by 'street parties and gifts of mugs, saucers and plates given to us by Hackney Borough Council on the Coronation of George VI in 1937, and completely unaware of Hitler'. Following a dose of chickenpox Billie was in need of recuperation. He himself takes up his story:

I was thin (like, I suspect, many East End kids) but not unhealthy. Wiry, my parents used to say. And I would play on the Marshes and by The Cut and by the River Lea so it must have been after one of the kiddies' illnesses that 'they' said I ought to go to a Convalescent Home because I was underweight. Yes, I can remember that but have no recollection of leaving my mum and dad and being transported to Brighton. So the authorities must have been quite skilful about prising me away from all I knew about the world – even my three-wheeler bike with the cardboard box tied on the back, in which I used to carry things about.

My memory [of St. John's] is vague but dark dormitories and iron bedsteads come to mind and the sort of hushed whispering of staff at night when we were put to bed. I feel that the staff were kind enough. I have recollections of young ladies in pale green overalls and helpers sweeping and cleaning and how one of the children 'told on me' for spitting (I think it was) in the washroom or toilets. The young lady listened to the tale of my misdemeanour, looked me in the eye and then just flicked water in my face from her wet hands. I got off very lightly.

…All the staff wore either pink or blue headwear, which reminded me of nuns' headwear… They would usher us into an awe-inspiring church, pinks on one side, blues on the other. I sat on the left looking towards the altar. The place was very hallowed and hushed and smelt of polish, extinguished candles and a sweet aroma – would that have been incense? I regret to say that I do not remember any of the sermons. I suppose that this would have taken place on Sundays.

One meal comes to mind, and that was sitting at a long table with other children and me having what I believe to be my first taste of lettuce. To me it was bitter and I did not like it. A girl with dark hair and a fringe just above her eyebrows offered to eat it for me, and as she was next but one to me we passed it behind the back of the intermediate child. It was a Cos type lettuce and would no doubt have been very good for me to eat. I wonder if that girl would be able to remember the incident?

Although it seems that our carers were nuns I have always thought of them as nurses and our best days were when they took us for walks in the country. Paths through green fields and hedgerows and fences, which we clambered onto and over. Even better when they took us to the beach for perhaps half a day and we paddled and collected the coloured 'gems' so beautiful when wet, which dulled as they dried. I never fail to

Edward Rudolf and The Waifs and Strays

In 1862 a Frenchman visiting London wrote in his diary, 'The whole place is alive with street-boys, bare-footed, filthy, turning cartwheels for a penny. They swarm on the stairs down to the Thames, more stunted, more deformed, more repulsive than the street-urchins of Paris.'[1] In fact in 1876, Dr Barnardo estimated that there were 30,000 children loose on the streets of London, 'living on their wits, stealing, begging, selling matches, moving from one rough shelter to another'. (This figure is all the more striking when compared to the 2017 estimate of 4,700 rough sleepers in London and 150 in

Edward Rudolf, founder of The Waifs and Strays, which later became The Church of England Children's Society. (The Church of England Children's Society)

Brighton.) Such crime, poverty and ill-health (there were four cholera outbreaks between 1846 and 1866) cried out for action.

Edward Rudolf (1852–1933), a largely self-educated Londoner, was both a church minister and a civil servant before taking on a further role as the superintendent of a Sunday school at St Anne's Church in Lambeth during the 1870s. When two of his most regular attenders suddenly stopped coming, he went in search of them and discovered them begging for food from workers at a neighbouring gasworks. Their father had died and their mother had left them to fend for themselves. He found the boys lodgings, in a home set up by Dr Barnardo. He and his brother Robert spent the next year, 1880, taking

soundings about setting up a home for destitute children to be run along strict Church of England lines demonstrating the Church in action, as opposed to the fiery doctor's more evangelical basis. He began with 14 founding fathers, who donated funds, and the Archbishop of Canterbury agreed to be President. His aim was to create for the children a family, rather than an institutional atmosphere.

The first home for girls opened in a rented house in East Dulwich in 1881, followed by another for boys in Clapton. Its growth was rapid: by 1890 there were 35 homes throughout the country looking after 1,600 children. By 1905 there were 93 homes and 3,600 children were being looked after, either in the homes themselves or with foster families. In 1946 the charity changed its name from the somewhat cumbersome Church of England Incorporated Society for Providing Homes for Waifs and Strays to The Church of England Children's Society; and in 1982 it became The Children's Society.

No homes exist now. The Society works with children and young people in need in local communities, with Local Authorities and in the youth justice sector.

St. John's association with the charity began formally in 1937 when it came under its auspices, although Sister Jane had correspondence with Prebendary Rudolf as early as 1910. It relinquished responsibility for the newly formed school in the early 1960s (see page 55).

---

1   Taine, Hippolyte, *Notes on England* (Thames and Husdon, 1957)

recollect that feeling inside me when I see a stony beach or children searching amongst the pebbles. I still, almost involuntarily, examine any that catch my eye.

Hot summer days and the smell of cabbages always bring to mind the day when us children were taken to a big house in its own grounds[8] where we were instructed to pick caterpillars off great crops of cabbages. They were, of course, cabbage white caterpillars and we were instructed to put them, thousands of them, into buckets. I do not have to tell you that myriads of caterpillars were constantly crawling up the sides of the buckets. What a day, and that unpleasant smell of cabbages is, again, a constant reminder of my convalescent days. I wonder what that house was and who the influential person was who was granted our child labour. The place was within walking distance of St. John's. I seem to remember that there was a walled garden.

…

My father would have been particularly concerned at my absence from the family home (my mother also but she could concentrate her energies on the other two) and it was he who, unannounced (I think) arrived to take me home. Remember, this was just before World War Two and minds must have been in a turmoil. The last thing a family wanted was to be separated. Dad arrived and I remember someone saying something to the effect that I should get ready as 'your father is coming for you'. What sweet words they were to me. He came into the office and lifted me onto the table and put my little black boots on and laced them up. His head was below and in front of me and I reached out to touch his head as if to make sure he was real.

He bought me some rock, all different colours in a cardboard boat, and we walked on the pebbly beach, where I found a silver shilling lying amongst the stones. A lot of money for a little boy in those days. And we came back to Hackney Wick via my grandfather's house in Holloway to my brothers and World War Two, when our family, like millions of others, were separated again. My convalescent time in Brighton remained a dark shadow in my mind…I am sorry to use that phrase, but that is how the building, pictured in the article,[9] seemed to me. Certainly the efforts [of the staff] are very much appreciated by me and, I suspect, many others who had some part in the history of the place.

…

So good old Miss Borradaile. Her good deeds led to better conditions for everyone. She and her likes probably laid the foundations for the National Health Service and improved social conditions all around.

In his final sentence Billy speaks for many. Shortly after his time at St. John's, in 1940, he was evacuated alone to a miner's household in Wales, 'having been separated from my elder brother Len in the Selection Hall, despite my mother's instruction that we should not be removed from each other – it was put right later when our teachers collected me and took me to join my brother staying with kindly Mrs Smith at Llanharry – but that's another story'. Quite apart from giving us a vivid picture of life at the Home just before

---

8   This is likely to have been Belle Vue Hall, to the south of St. John's. It was originally lived in by William Percival Boxall, from whom Sister Jane bought land to build the Home. It was demolished in the late 60s to make way for a block of flats, Belle Vue Court. The flint garden wall is still there.

9   An article on St. John's Home that appeared in the *Brighton and Hove Parochial Gazetteer* in the late 1930s, i.e. at the time of his stay, that Billy had clearly been sent.

The south face of St. John's. (St. John's College)

the outbreak of war, Billy's account is remarkable for the clarity of its observations after some 60 years (he wrote it in 1996), most strikingly the wet stones on the beach and the silver shilling (which perhaps his father had placed on the shingle for him to find).

In the late 30s business continued pretty much as usual and St. John's maintained its gentle way of life. Matron's Log is a day-by-day account of the events that mark any school year (regular nature walks, a recitation of Matthew Arnold's 'The Forsaken Merman' in December 1937, the illnesses that children in any boarding community fall victim to – e.g. 'The West Wing are in quarantine for German measles' in October 1938 – and regular days off). Partly because of the influence of the Sisters and the centrality of the chapel, Holy Days became holidays. In common with most schools, Ascension Day was a day off, but so was St Peter's Day on 29 June, Michaelmas Day on 29 September, All Saints Day on 1 November and so on. Interestingly, on 8 March 1939, Miss Cooper and Miss Lindo attended a course of Air Raid Precautions (ARP) lectures, preparing themselves, presumably, for the eventuality of war.

On 6 September 1939 the children had the first change to their routine as a result of war with Germany being declared just a few days earlier. Matron's Log reads: 'Owing to an air raid warning, given at 8.10am till 9.05am, it was not possible to begin school before 10.10am.' This was another routine that the children would easily adapt to, but

Muntham House, to which 30 children from St. John's were evacuated from March 1941 to July 1942. (With thanks to Muntham House School)

Whitehanger, a permanent wartime retreat in a 'delightful country house standing in 50 acres'. (With thanks to Lynn Paynter)

The eastern part of Brighton suffered particularly badly in September 1940 as bombers targeted the Kemp Town Gas Works, or shed their loads before making their way back across the channel. (Royal Pavilion and Museum, Brighton and Hove)

their parents became increasingly anxious about their children remaining on the coast, and began to withdraw them, which meant in turn that members of the teaching staff had to be laid off because there was simply not enough work for them. Whereas in 1939 305 children were admitted to St. John's, 56 boys and 249 girls, with an average stay of 88 days, by 1941 admissions of convalescent children had slumped to only 101 (24 boys and 77 girls). In September 1940 there were 16 air raid warnings and on the 14th a lone Dornier bomber dropped 20 100-pound bombs on Kemp Town, two of them hitting the Odeon Cinema killing four children and two adults. The committee had been trying, without much initial success, to find a house inland that could temporarily accommodate St. John's. Matron's Log entry for 24 March 1941 reads: 'The school, under orders of the Ministry of Health, evacuated to Horsham, to the estate of "Muntham", five miles from the town.' Mrs Upton, the owner of the substantial neo-Tudor house, had made available accommodation for 30 children. This was not in the house itself, but in one of two camps, already set up in the grounds for evacuated children from London schools. The house was occupied around this time by Canadian troops, which probably accounted for the St. John's children being moved again in July 1942 to Rozeldene, near Handheld, for four months. (In 1991, during the construction of a new building at Muntham, now a school not dissimilar to St. John's, an ammunition dump was unearthed, thereby halting work whilst bombs were defused. Perhaps it was as well that the children moved when they did.) Then their third wartime home, from October 1942, was Whitehanger, Marley Common, near Haslemere, 'a delightful country house standing in 50 acres'.

The war barely interfered with school routines. On 22 June 1943, Dr Bywater, the HMI, made her customary visit: 'She inspected books, handwork, wild flower collections, the work of the art class, etc. She was present at a Senior Singing Class and also at the Juniors' Singing and Percussion Band class.' The children did their bit for the war effort. 'Madam Alvin (Mrs Robson) cellist came to play for three quarters of an hour. A collection for the Navy League raised eleven shillings and eight pence.' Matron's Log notes that on 8 and 9 May the School was closed for VE Day. It was also closed the following day for Ascension Day, and the following two days for half term.

Chapter 7

Post-war: cold lamb and beetroot for lunch

O N 31 OCTOBER 1945 the School returned to Brighton. With 273 admissions, 39 boys, 234 girls and a surplus in the year (1945/46) of £1,132, St. John's was back to a healthy state. Early in 1948, a legal wrangle arose over who owned and ran the School. The Management Committee, as it had become known since the handing over to The Church of England Children's Society (CECS, formerly The Waifs and Strays Society), was composed of representatives of the CECS Executive Committee, chaired by Colonel Wyndham, and the St. John's Local Committee, chaired by Mr HC Mileham. Difficulties began when Sister Helena Mary offered the Home to the CECS in September 1937. She was in a hurry to get out and did not pursue the legal channels necessary for the Charity Commissioners to formulate a new schedule for the Home. The war intervened, the Home was evacuated and the issues surrounding the legality of the charity were forgotten. On 10 February 1948 it was agreed that Col Wyndham should assume the chair for joint meetings of the St. John's Board of Management and the Executive Committee of the CECS. Thereafter, the presence of the Chairman of the Home Committee and the Chairman of the CECS Executive Committee at such joint meetings led to difficulties that were to run for another 12 years, sometimes acrimoniously. The moral of this complex narrative is not to ignore the details when transferring a charity. One less contentious issue that such meetings addressed was the raising of Isabel Green's Matron's salary from £250 to £360 per annum; a 45% increase would have pleased her.

During the winter of 1950/51 Brighton experienced a smallpox epidemic. The disease was apparently brought in by a

All children at St. John's would have been issued with a ration book to allow the Home to buy their food during the war years. (The National Archives, UK)

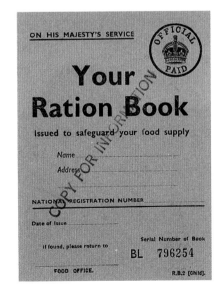

seaman whose ship had docked at Shoreham and who had lodgings in Brighton. At the Home, the Medical Officer (Dr Mary Price) required all staff to be vaccinated before the January term began, together with all children who had not been recently vaccinated. No case developed in the Home, the Board report tells us, 'but a child diagnosed as having had Scarlet Fever had to be isolated in the Home as the Public Isolation Hospital [at Bevendean, where the seaman had been sent] was in quarantine and reserved for smallpox cases'. This child was Ann, who gives this account of her time at St. John's:

In the Autumn of 1950, aged 9, I was admitted to the Radcliffe Infirmary at Oxford for a routine tonsillectomy. I was sent home 2 days later, but subsequently suffered a severe secondary haemorrhage. I was re-admitted for further surgery.

I am told that I never really recovered from this. It was recommended that I was sent to St. John's Home for Convalescents, and this occurred on 1st January 1951. Two days before I was due for admission it was learned that a member of the armed forces who had returned to Brighton from Aden had died of smallpox. I therefore had to have a smallpox inoculation. My parents took me, by train, via Paddington. I had never been parted from them before, and was desolate when they left. Within 2 days of admission it was discovered that the sore throat which had been troubling me since I arrived, was actually a symptom of scarlet fever (the skin peeled off my hands and feet too) which meant isolation in a tiny attic bedroom; another small girl was already there. We were kept there for 6 weeks, and although parents were normally allowed to visit once a month mine were not allowed to visit me during this time because of the risk of infection. I remember the one very kind nurse (because she had grey hair, I though of her as elderly) called Nurse Timworth. She only came to bring me food and bath us. It was very boring and I remember thinking 'This must be home-sickness'.

After this I settled into the routine of the Home. It appeared to be run largely by nuns,[10] and we had to visit Chapel twice daily. We were given pieces of triangular material, which when folded and buttoned at the back made a kind of headdress, which we had to wear in Chapel. My group wore blue headdresses and the others wore pink. We never saw them on any occasion other than when they attended Chapel. We had lessons every morning; I remember sitting doing my lessons on the upstairs balcony with my coat on because the windows were all open.

During the afternoons we would be taken for a walk, either along the seafront or up on the downs. I remember there was a brewery nearby,[11] and to this day I cannot bear the smell of malt. Every day after lunch we would have to queue up to have a spoonful of Virol. Luckily, I liked it, but many girls certainly did not. Lunch every Sunday consisted of cold lamb, a jacket potato and beetroot. I still can't eat any of those items. I guess some nutritionist had worked out that it was full of everything needed to fatten us up! Once a week, sweets were doled out; when our parents sent parcels for us, they were opened by the nuns, pooled, and then shared out amongst us. In retrospect this was

10 The Sisters of the Holy Cross Community had in fact left in 1937. Ann may, as a nine year old, have been confused by the headdresses the nurses wore, mistaking them for nuns' wimples.

11 The Kemp Town Brewery stood at the corner of Sutherland and Eastern Roads. It was demolished in 1971 and its site is now part of Brighton College.

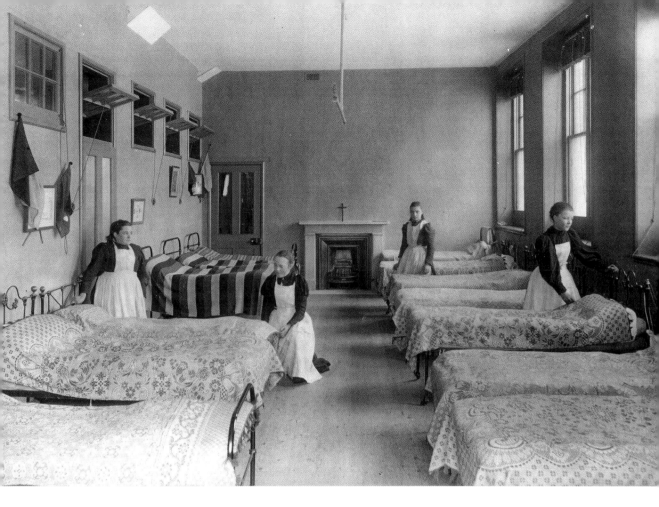

probably fair, as due to economic circumstances, some children never received parcels. We were not allowed to ask for anything – even toothpaste – we had to tell the nuns that. Neither were we allowed to seal the envelopes [when writing home]; the nuns censored the contents.

The photo of the dormitories is exactly how I remember them; the bed linen was changed every Wednesday, and our freshly laundered clothes would be placed in a neat pile on the end of the bed. The only time they were not there was if you were due to go home the following Saturday, so you would have to wait until then to put your clean clothes on! As you were never told when you would be going home, every Wednesday saw a big rush to see whether you had clothes on the end of your bed.

Just before my birthday on 18 May 1951, the lack of clean clothes on the end of my bed brought unimaginable joy! My parents collected me, and I returned home and to the village school that I had attended prior to St. John's. Despite a part-time education there, I managed to pass an entrance examination to a girls' grammar school. My health has been excellent since, no doubt due to Brighton's bracing air, and all those jacket potatoes! Although 70 now, I still do a 30-minute power walk before breakfast every day.

Sixty-seven years on Ann speaks warmly of the care she received from the kindly Nurse Timworth:

A typical dormitory. Such a uniform arrangement of beds, as in a hospital ward, was common in all boarding establishments until the late 1980s, when children were afforded more private space. (St. John's College)

Left: Ann, shortly after her six-month convalescence in 1951. (With thanks to Ann)

Right: Ann, with her husband John, on her first visit back to St. John's in March 2018. (St. John's College)

She was most kind to me, bringing me drawing paper and crayons (probably paid for out of her own pocket, as she felt so sorry for me). She also gave me a cuddle each night…I remember on one occasion being taken by car to the dentist. This was in a large black and white house some way north of the school. The dentist, I think, was a military man and unused to dealing with children. He decided I needed a filling in one of my front teeth, which he proceeded to do. When I looked in the mirror I was horrified to see that he had filled the tooth with a black filling. On my return home my parents immediately took me to our own dentist to have this work corrected.

In March 1950, the Ministry of Education granted Miss Lindo an extra six months' engagement as Headmistress from her 65th birthday in the following July. In April, Miss Madge Walker from Wembley Park was appointed Headmistress from September. The remuneration she was entitled to under the Burnham Scale was £534 (including the increment for Special Children). There is no record of what Miss Lindo's retirement salary was. In April 1951 Miss Green's salary as Matron was increased again, this time to £425 per annum.

The dynamic between the Headmistress and Matron in this period is open to some conjecture. Although the former was still paid more than the latter, it is noticeable that Miss Green attended meetings of the Board of Trustees and Miss Walker did not. Furthermore, in the case of a teacher who was alleged to have smacked a child in

October 1951, it was Miss Green who was asked to inform the teacher that she retained the full confidence of the Board, not the Headmistress. We can deduce then that Miss Walker was responsible for all timetabling and teaching matters, whilst Miss Green oversaw staff welfare and discipline as well as day-to-day matters of maintenance. It was certainly Miss Green who had to address the joint resignations of both the cook and her assistant in March 1952. There can be no doubt that Miss Green was the most significant figure in the Home during this era, following in the steps of Sister Jane Borradaile and Sister Helena Mary. 'The happy atmosphere of the Home is entirely due to the willing cooperation of the Matron, Miss Green, and the staff', the minutes of a meeting in the mid-50s tells us. Throughout this period the Home was relatively untroubled by major incident. Exterior painting, roof repairs, chapel restoration, the state of the staff flat at 42 Walpole Road and the purchase of a new lawn mower are recurrent items in the minutes of the Trustees' meetings.

In January 1955 Dr Mary Price resigned as Medical Officer of the Home in order to take up a full-time appointment with Brighton Education Authority. It was generally felt by the committee that 'the appointment of a lady doctor was to be preferred as her successor', but if a suitable lady should not be found 'then the qualifications of Dr C Black seem to meet the committee's requirements'. In the event, at the following meeting in March Dr Enid Fisher was duly appointed, with an honorarium of £60 per annum.

Throughout this period numbers were declining, with the result that finances were in a less than healthy state. For example, in July 1955 Mr Yarnell, the Treasurer, reported an excess of expenditure over income for the half year of £1,433, compared with a surplus of £120 for the same period of the previous year. In a Special Meeting on 23 April 1956, the Chairman referred to the declining need for vacancies in children's convalescent homes run by charitable institutions and then reported that it had been proposed by Headquarters (of the CECS) that 'the committee should consult with headquarters on the advisability of changing the Home's work to that of a residential school for educationally sub-normal children'. The committee agreed that circumstances were unlikely to change and the CECS welcomed the opportunity to place a number of their children currently in other homes in St. John's. It was unanimously agreed that Col Birnie, the Secretary of the CECS, should take up the matter with the Ministry of Education. Things moved swiftly thereafter: the Convalescent Home would close its doors at the end of October, and a residential school for sub-normal children aged 5–11 should open in January 1957, with Mr Ronald Chetwyn Butler as Headmaster. Miss Green took a lease on a flat from August in expectation of her retirement. The Home resolved to reimburse her the rent on this for three months.

Matron's Log for 31 October 1956 states: 'St. John's Home, School of Recovery for Delicate Children, closes at the end of this month. The last registration was for the morning session yesterday 30 October 1956.' Thus ends the first phase of St. John's history after 126 years, with the retirement of Miss Green.

Part II

St. John's History

Chapter 1

From home
to school

Aftera two-month hiatus in its history, St. John's re-opened in January 1957 as St. John's Residential Special School. By the mid-50s, the widening embrace of the National Health Service led to a lower demand for charity-run convalescent homes or special institutions for crippled children, and of course the demand for domestic servants had been declining since the end of the First World War. The special nature of the education offered by the School was for those who were 'educationally sub-normal' in the recognised parlance of the day, or ESN. In a less judgmental age we now refer to Special Educational Needs, or SEN. Just a slight shift of the letters in the acronym indicates a much greater shift that has taken place in educational attitudes over the past 60 years.

A shift too had taken place in the way St. John's was funded. No longer was it dependent upon ideals of Victorian munificence and charitable giving; it was now a state-funded school. A letter from the Ministry of Education at the end of 1956 confirms 'their approval pro tem of an annual fee of £348 for each child in the school'. Local Education authorities would direct children with special needs to the School; the Headmaster, Mr Chetwyn Butler, would negotiate with the LEAs the fees payable in order for the School to accept the children they recommended. In the event there were 42 admissions on 21 and 22 January 1957.

Children were presented with a television in 1958. Note the primitive wiring arrangements, which would certainly fall foul of modern Health and Safety Regulations. (St. John's College)

The new Board of Managers met on 14 January 1957, with Mr Tom Berry in the chair, Harry Mileham having resigned as Chairman, after serving St. John's in its previous incarnation for ten years; he agreed to re-join the Board as a member. Naturally enough, the Headmaster wanted changes to be made to accommodate these 42 five- to 11-year-olds safely, for example by installing new playground fencing and swings, and new school furniture, as about one third of the current furniture was in urgent need of replacement. A new school uniform (which would not be included in the fees, but charged separately to the LEAs) was decided upon: the boys' uniform cost £2 5s and the girls' £4 14s.

A number of staff changes occurred: Madge Walker had already left with the advent of a new head and others chose not to carry on with the School in its new form. Another resignation came shortly afterwards, in May 1957, when Bill Peters, chaplain of Brighton College, stood down from the chaplaincy of the School. Three months earlier, he had proposed making an *ex gratia* payment to a nurse[12] who was retiring after 22 years at the School, but was not entitled to a pension. The Board decided against making her any such payment. Harsh treatment, one might suggest after such a period of service, but equally it suggests how tight the finances of the School were in the post-war era. Under Chetwyn Butler's leadership the numbers rose by almost 50% to 61, and the possibility of opening an 11+ school was also mooted, but not actually implemented until after his time as Headmaster.

Throughout this early period of its existence as a specialist school, the School had two masters, the Ministry of Education, which was relied upon for funding major capital projects, and The Church of England Children's Society (CECS), under whose auspices St. John's had been run since 1937. It was decided at that time not to go to the Charity Commissioners for a definite scheme (known now as a memorandum of understanding), but for certain of the existing Trustees to retire in favour of Trustees who would be drawn from members of the Executive Committee of The Children's Society. The Sisters had stated their wish to retain the church connection and asked

Sir Frank Keith Officer, Chairman of the CECS, by Walter Stoneman, 1952. (© National Portrait Gallery, London)

the Society to frame rules for the management of St. John's on the general lines of the Society's rules for its other homes and schools. With the intervention of the war these rules were never officially drawn up. Indeed, the informal way in which this arrangement was set up before the war in 1937 came to be a source of regret for both Tom Berry, the St. John's Chairman, and Sir Keith Officer, the distinguished Australian diplomat, who in retirement was Chairman of The Children's Society.

Minutes and correspondence in the late 50s reveal accusations and counter-accusations that become acrimonious. Essentially, the School resented the CECS continuing to have any say in its day-to-day running (for example, the Headmaster wanted the CECS to play no part in staff resignations or appointments) whilst the CECS saw its branch in Brighton (i.e. the School) as a troublesome member of the organisation that needed to be kept in line. 'If I were Mr Berry I think I should begin to feel it necessary

---

12   This was Nurse Timworth, whom Ann had spoken so warmly of in 1951 (see page 48).

to watch my step', the Clerk to the CECS Trustees wrote to another Trustee in December 1959 after a sharp exchange of views. The joint meetings of the two bodies, held alternately in London and Brighton, were not always harmonious affairs. A letter from Mr Pick (a CECS Trustee) to Sir Keith in December 1960, following a joint meeting at the Ministry of Education, complains:

> It was quite obvious that there was a close understanding between Kemp Town and the Ministry and evidently much prior spadework had been done. Mr Vaughan and I were almost silenced if we attempted to intervene in the discussions and the Ministry chairman stated on more than one occasion that she was not interested in private feuds. This strengthened my belief that there is a pretty close collaboration between the Ministry and Kemp Town.

The discussion was over the matter of funding for the Headmaster's House, for which the Ministry was to supply funding.

The Editor of the *Brighton Herald* issues an apology. (St. John's College)

The ill-feeling was fuelled further in October 1960 by an article about St. John's in the *Brighton Herald* suggesting that the Society 'supported' St. John's. This led to an angry exchange of letters. 'An abominable imputation not to be tolerated by any normal parents' is the language used by the Chairman to Col Birnie (Secretary of the CECS) in what might be considered to be an overreaction to a perfectly innocent mistake on the part of the newspaper. Eventually, a correction appeared in the *Gazette* and gradually the uneasy relationship with The Children's Society petered out altogether. The new Rules for the Management of St. John's SEN School, worked on for so long through so many drafts, were finally agreed and published in January 1964 with no mention of The Children's Society, and so a 27-year association came to an end.

During this period two building projects occupied much of the Board's time: one was the building of a house for the Headmaster (mentioned above) on land to the east of the School that had been recently acquired; and the other was the conversion of the cottage, previously used by Heffernan, a handyman who is referred to by no other name, to teaching space. By 17 July 1962, the Ministry eventually settled on funding the cottage conversion at £2,130 and the house at £4,800.

In their new house the Butlers and their successors were to enjoy some of the best views in Brighton through the huge picture windows, typical of 1960s design. The house was to serve its purpose for 30+ years before being converted to student accommodation in 1992.

Meanwhile, the displaced Heffernan was compensated by an increase in his wages of £3 per week to £11 5s. He was also given a loan of £150, repayable over three

The Headmaster's House. (St. John's College)

years, to enable him to put down the deposit on a flat.[13] A further staff accommodation issue had been finding housing for the Deputy Headmaster. Various possibilities in the nearby Belle Vue Gardens fell through, but the new house for the Headmaster meant that his former quarters could now be used by his deputy.[14]

In 1962 the fees, which were paid by the LEA for the area the children came from, rose to £380 per annum, and the leaving age rose to 13. In 1966 the School was shocked by the sudden death of its Headmaster at the age of 45. At an emergency meeting of Governors on 14 September, 'Members stood in silence as a mark of respect to the late headmaster, Mr RC Butler'. It was arranged that Miss Moppet would take over as Acting Head pending the appointment of a successor. The minutes say further that Dr WG Stone, Director of Education for Brighton, had very kindly offered to consider all applications independently and prepare a short list. His kind offer was gratefully accepted. It was also later agreed that a letter of sympathy should be sent by the Governors to Mrs Butler, and a donation of five guineas be sent to the National Association for Mental Health.

The Acting Head's Report of October 1966 states: 'Pupils were told of the Headmaster's death on the first evening of term, and after some initial questions and discussions no further reference has been made and the children have accepted the fact well and are well adjusted to the situation.' And a few lines later, Miss Moppet records: 'During the first weekends of term several houses went blackberrying; some of the fruit was cooked for the children by the kitchen, the remainder being used by the cookery group for Bramble Jelly.' One senses here a welcome return to normality in the lives of the children and the staff after these upsetting events.

The reader may find it surprising that throughout this period there is virtually no mention of the education the children of St. John's received. Deliberations at Board level, as we have seen, were taken up with the question of who should run the School and with building projects and the sad matter of dealing with the untimely death of a headmaster. The actual education and welfare of the ESN children for whom the School existed seems to have been given less prominence. However, it would be far more central in successive eras.

---

13   Happily, the school did not forget Heffernan in his retirement: in October 1969, following Harvest Festival, 'a basket of fruit was sent to Mr Hefferman' (the first time in the annals of St. John's that he is accorded a 'Mr'!)

14   Mr SA Slowman, who had come from a secondary modern school in Worcester.

Chapter 2

The Forster years

T HE SECOND HEADMASTER of the new St. John's Special School was Mr Dennis Forster. He led the School from April 1967 (after a two-term interregnum) until December 1993. Thus at nearly 26 years he served for the longest period since the 43-year tenure (32 of them on the Walpole Road site) of Sister Jane Borradaile. He is unique among the Heads in that he kept a record of time in the form of a diary, which is of inestimable value for the historian.

Much of the material he recorded concerns the minutiae of school life, arrivals and departure of pupils and staff, individual Governor visits, trips and outings, minor disciplinary matters and pupil successes, all of which help to build a picture of a busy and thriving community.

Dennis Forster, St. John's longest-serving Headmaster, who served from 1966 to 2003. (St. John's College)

128 Eastern Road. St. John's moved here in to enable an extensive programme of refurbishment to take place at Walpole Road. (With thanks to the Regency Society)

This was a period of rapid development for the School, both in terms of numbers, which rose to 80 by 1970, and improvement and extension of the premises. For the academic year 1972–73 the whole school (apart from the kitchen and laundry) relocated down the hill to Eastern Road to allow the building to be totally refurbished and modernised. The work was funded in the main by the Department for Education. Dennis Forster writes that the children settled down 'amazingly quickly' in their new building, 'which in many ways is more suitable than the Walpole Road premises'. The new building in question was 128–136 Eastern Road, which had recently been vacated by Brighton College Junior School, before their move across the road to Walpole Lodge.

Certainly, there were fewer stairs for the children to negotiate and it was nearer to the sea. All went well there and morale was high. 'It has been gratifying to see the general improvement in the happiness and well-being of the pupils this term. It is also obvious that the House Matrons are much more relaxed and confident in their work.'[15]

In common with a general shift in attitudes towards parents in boarding schools, this was a period when visits to the School were welcomed and encouraged. At Open Days at half term, for example, parents were permitted for the first time to take their children home with them afterwards. There was also an open invitation to official bodies: most of the 19 LEAs who sent children to St. John's visited the School and were impressed with what they saw, as were Heads of other schools. The local branch of the Soroptimists visited in 1982 and pledged to raise £1,000 for the School, which was used to buy BBC microcomputers. Nine educational psychologists visited in Spring Term 1983. There is a

15   This comment needs to be seen in the context of the previous year, which was something of an *annus horribilis* for the school, following the sudden death of a master. Dennis Forster's final comment that summer term was: 'This has been a difficult and very sad term for all of us.'

sense in this period that St. John's was looking to lead the field in the kind of specialist education it offered by showing visitors or former pupils what it was doing.

Dennis Forster was active in the community – he was a JP and had a wide circle of acquaintances – encouraging local schools to make St. John's a part of their community service programme. A boy from Brighton, Hove and Sussex Grammar School writes of his visits at this time:

> The interior of the School has been redecorated and fitted with modern teaching aids and now provides new, clean living accommodation for all concerned… Many of the children come from miles away, usually from broken homes or large families where the parents cannot give them the extra time, patience and care they require. All of them enjoy life at the School, rather sadly, perhaps, some of them prefer it to living at home.

He goes on to speak of the varied progress that the children make. This is perhaps a simplified schoolboy's account, but nevertheless it gives a picture of a busy and happy school.

One of the major developments in facilities in Dennis Forster's first ten years was the construction of a learner swimming pool, over which Foundations (a maintenance skills workshop) now stands. This was opened by Alan Mullery, Manager of Brighton and Hove Albion FC, in April 1978.

In January of that year, The Variety Club of Great Britain presented a minibus to the School. An *Argus* photograph shows its gleeful reception by the children (and their Headmaster).

Visits beyond the school became prolific. In January 1979 there were trips to London to see *Toad of Toad Hall, Peter Pan* and *Joseph*. This was in addition to the various theatre and music groups that visited the School. Certainly, children were becoming

On a dark January day, Air Commodore Freddie Milligan presents Dennis Forster and gleeful children with a minibus on behalf of The Variety Club of Great Britain. (St. John's College)

Dog shows

Dennis and Gaynor Forster were dog lovers and owned bull terriers, which were part of the extended St. John's family. In the 1970s they conceived the idea of holding an annual dog show during the summer term, partly for fund-raising purposes and also as a PR exercise. The shows were certainly successful in entertaining the children and bringing into the School those who would otherwise not be aware of it. Dogs were brought from all over Sussex to these 'Exemption Shows', which allowed for a broader range of dogs than the more specialised 'Pedigree Shows'.

Les Crawley of BBC Radio Brighton hosted a programme, *All About Dogs*, from 1971 to 1993 and used it to advertise the St. John's Show in the Diary Dates feature. A regular guest on the programme was local vet Tony Cowie, who was a judge from the mid-70s to the mid-80s, as was his colleague Duncan Blackburn on occasions. The afternoon would always begin with a lunch for judges and Governors, given by the ever-hospitable Forsters in their house above the School. After strawberries and cream the show, and the judges' work, would begin, the children running to and fro with cups of tea for them.

Dog show official's badge.
(Photograph by Liz Coles, St. John's College)

This was not just a dog show; it was also a fete. Side stalls selling cakes and other produce abounded. Dennis himself was master of ceremonies, welcoming visitors, congratulating winners and directing operations. In this, as in so many other ways, he was a hands-on Headmaster. The event reached its apotheosis on Saturday 21 June 1975, the centenary of the founding of St. John's. Stanley Dangerfield, who presented Crufts for the BBC for many years, agreed to be a judge, a troupe of Morris dancers and a marquee were booked. It was a great success and attracted over 400 entries.

Tony Cowie believed that if it hadn't been for the dog shows, many would not have heard of St. John's; and what a lovely community occasion they found, with well-behaved children, welcoming staff and literally hundred of dogs!

Dog show programmes.
(St. John's College)

more and more aware of the world beyond Walpole Road. Furthermore, the celebrated annual dog show (see page 60) brought many further visitors to St. John's.

At the end of 1980, a new venture was proposed and 13 Walpole Road was purchased from Hamilton Lodge to become a unit for ten 13–16 year olds requiring special care. Borradaile House duly opened in January 1982.

Julie Newson was appointed as a House Matron in September 1978, which involved working in one of the dormitories, looking after between eight and ten children before and after classes, overnight and at the weekends. She was thus heavily involved in the pastoral life of St. John's. Now the Rev Julie Newson, she is Deacon at St Luke's Church, Brighton. She recalls her time at the School:

> In 1982, I was privileged to be asked to be in charge of Borradaile House, 13 Walpole Road. No expense was spared in setting it up and it became the show house for the school. The beds were hand-made on the Freshfield estate, the kitchen was kitted out with crockery, cutlery and very expensive saucepans from the David Mellor shop in Knightsbridge, and Philip Dunn, the local artist, visited to decide which of his pictures should hang in which part of the house.
>
> There were additional extras, such as a beautiful wooden fruit bowl, wooden napkin rings with names carved on them, wooden names on the bedroom doors, making the whole place feel very special and a quality provision that was far superior to most school boarding houses of the time, and now!
>
> Dennis Forster's wife, Gaynor, was behind this and her influence throughout his headship should not be underestimated. They were both very involved with the young people at Borradaile. They would join us for many of their meals and

Borradaile House in the 1980s. 'Gaynor Forster made the place feel very special with a quality of provision that was far superior to most school boarding houses of the time, and now!' (Ian Muir Photographer)

Dennis and Gaynor
Forster in the window
of Seaview. (St. John's
College)

would arrange and lead outings to London: shopping in Covent Garden and Harrods, theatre trips and eating out in smart restaurants.

At St. John's, Mr Reg Golden, the carpenter/maintenance man, was given a pay rise and told always to prioritise Borradaile; and Mrs Doreen Wareham, who looked after the Headmaster's house and provided exemplary catering for special occasions, was also briefed to look after Borradaile in the same way.

Few people were able fully to take on the philosophy of surrounding children, who were often deprived and with special needs, with beautiful (and expensive) resources, but it did have a very special feel to the place.

I lived in Borradaile House for 13 years, until I was promoted to a senior care position, with an office in the main school building in 1995.

This was indeed a time of boom. By September 1983, Dennis Forster was able to write: 'The character of the school has changed: there are more, older pupils [11–13] at St. John's, who are academically of a higher standard. A special dormitory has been provided for the girls, with better furniture and equipment.' It was now very full (86 pupils with one being a day pupil).

On the last day of the Spring Term 1984, Dennis Forster was informed that there was to be an HMI Inspection in early May. Nothing in the School world focuses the minds of heads and staff quite like a school inspection, and the Easter holidays would have been a time of feverish preparation to ensure that criteria were met and documentation prepared.

Unsurprisingly, the inspectors commented on 'the excellent relationships between staff and children – remarkable for their warmth, friendliness and happiness'. There were criticisms, of course: the extension of the age range had put pressure on accommodation; assessments were rather subjective; and record keeping a little arbitrary. These criticisms led the School to address the recommendations. Heads often needed the spur of Inspection recommendations for leverage with the Governors. Amongst other things, four new classrooms were created and the School was reorganised into three clear sections, each containing classes grouped according to ability.

In late June 1989, a life-changing event occurred in the life of Dennis Forster: 'My wife died the day before the Dog Show, but it was her wish to continue with it.' And indeed the show did go ahead, in this most testing of circumstances, telling us much about Dennis Forster's loyalty to St. John's. He and Gaynor had lived the life of the School for the past 22 years, treating the pupils as their extended family, and taking a great interest in every aspect of their personal welfare. They took much pride in their uniform, for example, decking them out in Barbour jackets and Hunter boots for outdoor wear. It is the stuff of legend that one of the duties teaching assistants were tasked with was to clean these boots when the need arose.[16] Thus, St. John's children were impressively well turned out. Gaynor, who served as Domestic Bursar, believed that being in the presence of beautiful things can help to transform young lives, as we see from Julie Newson's account above. She had just celebrated her 60th birthday at the time of her death. The Board minutes from 12 July record: 'The Headmaster informed Governors that he intended to continue as Headmaster and as far as was humanly possible, he would maintain the high standards previously achieved, largely by Mrs Forster's influence in the school.'

The year 1991 saw the opening of the new classroom block, now known as Pier View and previously AVOC, north of the original building. It comprised seven classrooms, including the highly successful Food Technology Room and the Art and Design Department. The building was opened on 7 March by Lord Tonypandy, the renowned Speaker of the House of Commons who began his career as a teacher, and who employed the current CEO's sister as his secretary.

Whilst these building works were in progress some teaching had to take place in two Portakabins, which made repeated appearances over the next 20 years as more and more additions were made to the St. John's site. Long-standing staff remember them almost with affection.

Also at this time there was concern about pupil numbers. Board minutes record that LEAs were not meeting their statutory obligations in respect of preparing statements of Special Educational Need, largely because of financial constraints. It was clear that the Department of Education was withdrawing active support from non-maintained special schools, such as St. John's. A first step to rectify this shortage would be to re-write the prospectus and to circulate it widely. In short, St. John's would advertise.

16   Interview with Dennis Boxall (a care assistant at the School), 9 April 2018.

Portakabins: 'Remembered almost with affection from the 1990s!' Note the absence of hard hats in a less H&S conscious age. (St. John's College)

Chapter 3

School and college

Following the retirement of Dennis Forster, Mike Hudson began his headship in January 1994. From the outset he knew that he was going to have his work cut out for him, taking over from a much-loved predecessor who had served the School for 26 years. It was immediately clear to his staff that things would be done very differently. Even his title was changed; from 1957 a Headmaster had run the School but now the post was to be titled Principal, 'in line with other schools', as he said in his first report to the Governors in March. It was a 'new model of management' that he headed himself. 'This group, incorporating an Administrative Officer, a Head of Education, a Head of Care and a Bursar meets fortnightly to discuss matters of strategic planning.' The very language used here speaks of a new approach to running a school, one that spread to all parts of the operation.

New policies were written on Behaviour Management, Health Care and Food, whilst others were fully revised. There was a renewed focus on what the School was for and

Mike Hudson, Headmaster 1994–2000. (St. John's College)

how the vision for a child-centred education was to be realised. This was enshrined in what would now be called a mission statement, which was presented to the Governors and the staff in June 1994:

> To provide a secure yet challenging physical and social environment in which children and young people can grow intellectually, emotionally, socially and spiritually. Young people who leave St. John's will demonstrate increased personal responsibility, social competence and intellectual curiosity.

From the outset, he wanted the School become a specialist centre; and he wanted it to be full. Richard Stewart, Chairman of the Trustees, recalls that numbers had slumped to only 54 before Mike arrived. As part of a drive to raise its profile, not only locally, but also regionally and internationally, Mike Hudson laid the foundations for a Professional Development Centre. This would operate in four categories: INSET, Publications, Consultancy and Inspection work. By July this had already taken off, with three INSET courses having taken place and six more in the pipeline.

He also wanted his school to be open to as broad a range of specialist needs as possible, which put a strain on all. Smith-Magenis syndrome, for example, is a developmental disorder that causes distinctive facial features. Those with the condition often have affectionate and engaging personalities, but also serious behavioural problems, including tantrums, aggression and impulsiveness. At one point during his time there were nine diagnosed with the condition in the School, a significant proportion of all the known cases in the country. One girl with an extreme case of the syndrome was required to leave after biting other students and throwing one of them down the stairs. Occasionally, life at St. John's could be challenging for staff and students alike. In spite of Mike Hudson's laudable aim to care for as many troubled children as possible, there were times when he had to bow to the only course of action open to a head, which is to pass an individual on to another institution for their own good and the welfare of the majority.

In the summer of 1995, the Principal took his senior team on an Away Day to discuss future plans for the School, which proved very successful. The minutes of the Board meeting that term tell us: 'The chairman applauded all the ideas thrown up by the Away Day Team and felt that the governors needed to match and contribute to the staff output.' This is a telling comment: no longer were governors mere benevolent observers of others' work; they were now going to emulate the staff in their determination to drive the School forward. To help them do this they elected to undertake training on governors' roles and responsibilities on a course designed by the Principal.

Dennis Boxall joined St. John's in March 1995, having been persuaded by Mike Hudson to take a career change and become a learning support assistant. He speaks of his new employer's warmth and approachability, and of how seriously he took caring for his students. On one occasion he drove a child home to Southampton after her behaviour had made it impractical for her to remain at the School. On arrival, the response of the mother indicated that she was clearly not welcome there. It says much for Mike Hudson's approach and instinctive sense of what is right that he put her straight back in the car and drove her back to school.

The most significant innovation in this era arose through the government's creation of the Further Education Funding Council, whose purpose was to allocate funds to individual students with special needs once they turned 16 and 19. Mike Hudson and his Chairman, Leon Morton, rapidly set about creating a scheme to create more space, which was detailed in a paper entitled 'Raising the Roof'. This was no educational metaphor about raising standards, but an actual scheme to add another storey to the School to accommodate 25 students, aged 19+, in three teaching bases – Home Economics, Horticulture and Technology. The cost of this was estimated at £225,000. In the event, it did not happen, partly through planning difficulties and partly because a building in Church Road that would make an ideal Further Education Centre became available on a short-term lease. Accordingly, in September 1996 the English Language Centre leased to St. John's three floors of their Hove premises at 35 Church Road. The new facility was run by Coral Romain. The unit provided continuing basic education, leading to nationally recognised qualifications – City and Guilds and the Further Education Youth Award Scheme. Study Skills programmes, Life Skills and Personal and Social Education were on offer to the 20 or so students who formed the first cohort.

In 1999, a property in Seaford was leased by the rapidly expanding St. John's (see chapter 4). A new company limited by guarantee was established, swiftly followed by a new charity, St. John's School and College. It was a requirement of the Further Education Funding Council that two governing bodies would now be required, one of Trustees and one of Governors, with a Chairman for each.

35 Church Road, Hove. This was St. John's Further Education Centre from 1996 to 1999, when it moved to the main campus in Walpole Road after Seaford was acquired as a base for the School. (St. John's College)

On the home front, in order to make the staffing more in keeping with college-aged students, or older learners, Mike Hudson cut down on the number of residential staff, most notably in Borradaile House and even moved his own family out of the Headmaster's House so that it could become the Business Centre, which more recently has become a residential home for young women called Pier View.

The Outlook Foundation began in January 1997, the idea having been originally conceived by Gaynor Forster, who had the vision; Jean Marshall, one of the Trustees, had the drive and Len Parkyn, the Chairman of the Governors, made the dream a reality. (Len moved on after 18 months to be head of Cherry Trees in Hove, a special needs FE Centre.) An independent charity, the mission of the Outlook Foundation is to 'empower people with learning disabilities by providing safe, comfortable homes in the community'. The three properties acquired were a vital bridge towards independent living for their residents.

So many changes in so short a space of time inevitably had an unsettling effect on some staff, although they could see that expansion and this reallocation of learners was good for the School and College as a whole. In July 1996, a Governor raised the question of staff and student stress. 'Mr Hudson was able to reassure his Governors', the minutes of the Board meeting state, 'that thought had been given to this and that counselling would be available'. His determination to continue to cater for those with the most challenging of needs, including those with Smith-Magenis Syndrome, continued unabated.

Sharon Jaque, who arrived at St. John's in 1996 to take over Art and Design and teach other subjects, identifies the complexity of the task of teaching learners with such special needs and such a range of abilities. 'Basic human skills such as living with other people and forming relationships may be taken for granted in mainstream schools, but are a major challenge here', she says. In her capacity as Head of Learning Support Services, Sharon became closely involved in training staff. One aspect of living together was that the learners were able to enjoy taking part in the annual Adventure Holidays to France (the Dordogne and Normandy). These breaks were initiated by Mike Hudson in the mid-90s, and continued for seven or eight years, latterly together with the Seaford School. They were hard work for the accompanying staff, but of great benefit to the children, and hugely enjoyable for all. Such visits continue to this day with European funding.

On leaving St. John's, Mike Hudson moved to Brighton Technical (now the City) College. In spite of his own jocular

Top: Outlook House, painted in 1996 by Jean Marshall. (With thanks to the artist)

Centre: Len Parkin, Chair of the Governors from 1983 to the present, with Liam H, a learner. (St. John's College)

Bottom: Richard Stewart, Chair of the Trustees from 1997 to the present. (St. John's College)

French trips in the 90s. 'Happy children on holiday.' These trips were hard work for the staff, but hugely enjoyable for all. They provided an opportunity for younger and older learners to spend time together. (St. John's College)

assertion that the place 'nearly broke me', his legacy to St. John's is a very considerable one. He raised the profile of the School and by extending the age range ensured that the increased revenue from greater numbers would sustain St. John's in the years to come. He inherited a school of 78 pupils and left it with 109. Len Parkyn speaks of his 'sincerity' and how his 'heart was always in the right place'.

Chapter 4

Seaford

IN THE MID-20TH century there were as many as 30 preparatory and private schools in Seaford, which is just down the coast from Brighton. Sadly, they are no more. However, one, the Pilgrims School for Asthmatics in Seaford, was acquired by St. John's in 1999 on a leasehold arrangement and was purchased five years later, £775,000 having been raised.[17] This enabled a reorganisation of the School and College: in due course all of the learners aged nine to 16 moved to Seaford whilst the Brighton site became the FE College for learners aged 16–19. This meant that the Church Road property was no longer needed. It made sense for older students to be based in Brighton, the increasingly vibrant city being a natural habitat for young people; whilst the gentler and more spacious Seaford environment, with its flat sports pitches and uncluttered playing areas, was more suitable

---

17   This purchase sum, £630,000, was calculated by adding an inflation quotient to the value of the property
     at the time the lease was taken out.

Princess Margaret opened the Pilgrims School (later St. John's Seaford) in 1955. Here she is shown arriving by helicopter for another visit. (Seaford Museum and Heritage Society)

The Hive, Seaford.
The *trompe l'oeil* on
the side of this block
immediately transports
the visitor ten miles to
the east to the Seven
Sisters. (Ian Muir
Photographer)

for younger pupils. A swimming pool and good-sized gym were also invaluable facilities
to inherit. Don Kent was the deputy appointed to run this new primary and secondary
school (for those aged 11–16), succeeded by Jane Molyneux after 2000.

Today, the overall atmosphere of the School is one of light and space, within which
a generous staffing ratio enables each individual's needs to be given due attention. A
sense of well-being pervades the School, recalling the 'bright, happy little family' that
Sister Jane wrote of 120 years ago when she first set up her Home in Walpole Road.

Sensory Learning at
Seaford. The Therapy
Room is the centre for
a 'sensory diet' for non-
verbal learners. (Ian
Muir Photographer)

As at Brighton, horticulture is an important part of the curriculum for learners at Seaford. (Ian Muir Photographer)

Seaford currently has 30 learners, mostly residential, who come from the Midlands and London, as well as Hampshire and Sussex. They are divided into three Pathways, reflecting the structure at the College, which most of them go on to at 19. In terms of pastoral care, learners are looked after in four houses, all of them on site, with three of them spread over three floors of the main building. An elaborate system of care staff for both day and night are there to look after them.

As at the College, some of the learners are non-verbal and the Therapy Room is the centre for a 'sensory diet'. The Picture Exchange Communication System (PECS) is a key part of the work that goes on there. This is a package that allows those with autism, and other communication difficulties, to initiate communication. PECS begins with teaching learners to exchange a picture of a desired object with a teacher, who immediately responds to the request. For example, if a learner wants a drink, they will give a picture of a drink to an adult who immediately hands them one. Verbal prompts are not used, thereby encouraging spontaneity. The system goes on to teach discrimination of symbols and enables learners to communicate reasonably fluently by constructing simple 'sentences'.

With an eye to employability, Young Enterprise flourishes at the School. Plants are grown in the Therapy Room, which are then sold in the open market in Brighton. Horticulture is also practised in the Polytunnels in the grounds.

Ellie Crosthwaite, Care Manager at the School, speaks of the way that School and College are now more joined up than ever before in her time there. Under Simon Charleton, the Chief Executive, the provision across the whole age range, from five to 25, is undeniably holistic.

Chapter 5

Millennials

DON KENT TOOK over as Principal from Mike Hudson in September 2000, having been a notably hard-working deputy at Walpole Road before running the School at Seaford. He was a technology teacher by training and understood instinctively the challenges facing his staff, though he had to learn how to respond to the needs of older students as well as how to lead a business that needed to keep moving forward, as it had done rapidly under his predecessor. He styled himself Chief Executive, but continued as a teacher for his first three years until the demands of headship took over. This was an age when regulatory measures meant that heads began to see themselves as running a business, not merely providing a first-rate education. Some of the more established staff may have raised an eyebrow at this elevation, especially when they saw less and less of their CEO as he was either busy with overseeing developments at Seaford or ensconced in his office in the Business Centre.

Don Kent, Chief Executive 2000–10. (St. John's College)

The Crypt Cafe in
St George's Church.
(St. John's College)

This was a very strong period financially, probably the strongest in the history of the School, in which considerable capital reserves, in the region of £2 million, were built up, thanks to the careful husbandry of Terry Chandler, the Finance Manager from 2003, who succeeded the long-serving Shelagh Heath.

Whilst less emphasis was placed on refurbishing and equipping the Brighton campus, a number of capital investment projects took place at Seaford. For example, the Hive block was built to provide teaching space and a large meeting room (see page 70). An ongoing concern of CEOs since 2000 has been how much time to devote to each site during the working week so as to allow learners and staff in each to feel included and valued. A considerable and lasting contribution made by Don Kent to the development of St. John's was to consolidate some of the changes that had come about in the previous five years, and in particular to make Seaford and Walpole Road feel part of the same organisation.

There are always times in a school when thought needs to be given to the basic principles of how pupils learn and what needs to be done to help them learn most effectively. As a practised teacher himself, Don Kent was well placed to re-think the curriculum and the way it was delivered. Accordingly, in the mid-2000s there was a move away from organisation in departments (English, Maths, Art, etc.) towards a grouping of Faculties. He established them as follows:

AVOC, the Faculty of Academic and Vocational Studies, was designed to meet the needs of learners aged 16–22, who had been assessed as having moderate but complex learning difficulties. The broad academic curriculum offered them the opportunity to prepare for independent adult lives by focusing on developing intellectual, social, emotional and physical skills. Staff had high expectations of this group and targets were set high. AVOC was overseen by Helen Grice and Martin Timmins.

Scrummies cafe. (Ian
Muir Photographer)

The **LINC** Faculty was about **L**iving together and working in a small group to develop **IN**dependent skills, and through interacting with each other to develop social and **C**ommunication skills for 'self advocacy'. A significant part of the curriculum was planned to take place outside the College, in the wider environment. LINC, the largest of the three Faculties, was set up and run with conspicuous success by Michelle O'Shea. Its focus was primarily on autism.

Scrummies cafe. Once
the School's dining
room, Scrummies is
now an extremely
successful and popular
cafe space. Many
learners work here to
acquire catering skills.
(St. John's College)

The Life Skills Unit was set up to meet the needs of learners with severe learning difficulties. The focus of the curriculum was the attainment of practical skills that could be transferred to their everyday lives and enable them to function as confidently and independently as possible. Linda Hogben ran this, whilst all three programmes were overseen by the Head of College, Coral Romain.

The Faculties were later replaced by Pathways, whereby learners are assigned to one of three learning groups based on their functional ability. They join a tutor group within a Pathway, which comprises a small number of peers with similar needs and a team of dedicated staff.

As well as these developments in the area of cognitive and social skills, Enterprise Education, which addressed the all-important question of equipping learners for the world of work, and later to become 'Work Related Learning', had three strands.

The Crypt Cafe was set up in the crypt of the nearby St George's Church. It was a real business owned by learners and staff and provided activities that supported and complemented what was done under the curriculum. This proved to be a long-term success and was re-born in 2013 as **Scrummies** in the basement of the main Walpole Road building. The name itself had existed previously to refer to the breakfasts (and some lunches, particularly popular with staff) that the learners from the Food Technology department prepared and marketed.

Flourish was established the year after **Scrummies**, although several of its activities had been in place previously under the name of **Greenfingers**. Learners worked on the care and maintenance of some areas of the College grounds, developing key skills at the same time.

Power Print started in January 2000 and provided a professional print and sign service. Using skills developed in ICT lessons, learners created letterheads, brochures, business cards, menus, etc. Its latest form is now to be found at **Inklusion** in Freshfield Road.

All of these enterprise activities still form the basis of today's co-curricular programme, although with different names and, like Scrummies, in different locations.

Learners working in the grounds. Horticulture (now termed Flourish) has long been a popular and very productive curricular activity at St. John's. (Ian Muir Photographer and St. John's College)

These changes and innovations required a certain reallocation of the space in Brighton. For example, after 30 years of use the learner swimming pool became used for Greenfingers until it was filled in to become a workshop and is now Foundations.

Development at the School in Seaford continued, particularly when it opened a sixth form in 2008 and began taking in learners aged 16 and above. This meant that for a time there was a sixth form crossover between the Seaford and Brighton campuses, until the natural movement of learners meant that the tertiary/higher educations lines could be clearly drawn.

Above: Montage of work from Inklusion. Inklusion, a very St. John's coining, is a successful business venture in nearby premises where leaners, guided by a professional staff team, can create a variety of products, among them the monthly newsletter, *St. John's Life*. (St. John's College)

Left: Learner working at Inklusion print shop. (St. John's College)

Chapter 6

A legacy of rare quality

MARK HUGHES ARRIVED in September 2010 and it was clear to anyone who met him that his mindset was commercial as well as educational. 'We need to spend to survive' was his instinct and without delay he set about spending the capital reserves that had accrued under his predecessor, who together with Terry Chandler had had a cautious approach to expenditure.

Trustees were of the view that a major overhaul of the fabric of St. John's was required. Some areas of the School had become virtual no-go areas for prospective parents. For example, ICT provision was rudimentary to say the least, not much different from Dennis Forster's innovations 20 years previously, and confined to one room. This was at a time when other institutions were forging ahead, parading newly installed smart boards in all classrooms.

There were Health and Safety issues too. Mark Ryan, the Employability Manager, recalls Mark Hughes being taken on an inspection tour of the site by Martin Timmins from the Business Development department within a few days of arriving. Walking down a narrow passage outside Seaview, Martin Timmins failed to notice that a swing window was wide open, having no stops. His forehead may well still bear the scar of that unfortunate encounter. In any event, this acted as the spur for Mark Hughes to correct a number of Health and Safety issues in order to become compliant as soon as possible with the requirements of the Disability Discrimination Act of 2010, which was just coming into force. A lift was essential, as were carefully placed handrails and markings on steps and elsewhere. Such expenditure was welcomed by the teaching staff, who were all too conscious of the threadbare nature of the furnishings, even if some members of the finance staff were reluctant to see so much money spent.

Mark Hughes, CEO/
Principal 2010–16.
(St. John's College)

Marketing became an integral part of the operation. From 2011, Len Parkyn, an active Trustee with extensive experience of SEN, was given the job of raising the profile of St. John's; within 18 months numbers were increased by one third, especially in the tertiary section at the College. Mark Hughes was a high-profile Head, warm-hearted and generous in his greeting of staff and learners, and was much present around the School during the working day; learners were made to feel special when interacting with him. Not a great deal of desk work got done during the school day – he worked at home in the evenings in his flat at the marina; his family was based on the Isle of Wight, to which he returned on Friday afternoons. However, at 5pm on a Sunday afternoon his working week in Brighton would begin again. In the words of Lucy Howells, now the Marketing Manager, who worked closely with him: 'He was a leader, not a manager. He empowered others to take projects forward and take due credit for them.'

When the Ofsted inspectors arrived in September 2012 they found that 'this provider was good' because:

> Many learners move on to supported living or further education or employment after they leave; Teachers use their knowledge and skills very successfully; Specialist therapists and teachers work together very effectively to identify learners' individual needs when they first join the college, and to develop their core skills right through to the time they leave; and the school is led and managed well.

It was judged not to be 'outstanding' because:

> The staff do not have sufficient skills and knowledge to provide good and impartial information, advice and guidance. The targets set for learners in

The College grounds. 'A thoughtfully designed and well-managed landscape that lifts the spirits.' (Ian Muir Photographer)

subject areas are not as clear and precise as they are for core skills. Not all staff use language and resources that are appropriate for the age of the young adults they teach and support.

Those who worked closely with Mark Hughes[18] remark on how he respected the learners in his charge as individuals with their own personalities, skills and strengths, and was passionate about supporting the aspirations and ambitions of each one to allow them to achieve their very best. He saw the School and College as special in their ability to give the learners a dignity and self-worth that in other environments, or certainly in previous generations, they would have lacked. What learners see as they walk around St. John's grounds today is a thoughtfully designed and well-managed landscape that lifts the spirits and creates a feeling of pride in the place that is their home for three years or more.

What was to become of learners after they left St. John's constantly preoccupied Mark Hughes and he believed passionately in work experience (as was recognised by the inspectors). This was no mere box to tick. He knew that his learners were going to have to overcome more obstacles than most to make their way in the world. He formed relationships with local businesses so that learners could feel that their needs were being seriously addressed. Inklusion, Harmonies, the musical cafe at Seaford, and Scrummies in Brighton, opened by Jane Asher in 2013, were places where students could work and learn basic skills and the principles of commerce, and he considered their development to be essential.

During his headship Mark Hughes relaunched and renamed a number of the enterprise projects that had existed since 2004, in an extension of the work-related learning scheme. Flourish succeeded Greenfingers in the care and preparation of the

18   Among them was Naomi Alder, the CEO's PA.

The 2013 opening of Scrummies, with Jane Asher. Richard Stewart, Chairman of the Trustees, and Mark Hughes, CEO/Principal, are enjoying their tea in the background. (St. John's College)

The logos of the various enterprises run by St. John's. (St. John's College)

Reveals, 2015.
'Learners could
convince themselves
for an hour or two that
they really were at a
Rock Festival...'
(St. John's College)

grounds; Inspirations became the in-house shop; Ability operated under the wing of the IT department; Solutions was stationery supplies and administration; Foundations was a workshop for simple maintenance skills; Productions was the hub of performing arts; Resonance gave access to musical performance and technology; and Shine has now become the new Domestic Services project. Each of these spheres of activity became defined by its own distinctive logo.

The staff enjoyed it too,
wearing t-shirts printed
by learners at Inklusion.
(St. John's College)

Learners enjoying the drumming workshop and performing on stage at the Reveals Festival, which formed part of the 130-year anniversary celebrations.
(St. John's College)

Mark Hughes wanted to make sure St. John's was 'out there', and he sought to do this in a number of ways. The bright and colourful logo was an initiative of his and he chose to make a promotional video for the website from the comfort of a multicoloured deckchair, incongruously wearing a three-piece suit. In the summer of 2015, he had the idea for the Reveals festival, where learners could convince themselves for an hour or two that they really were at a rock festival on the Isle of Wight.

He established Graduation in 2012, a ceremony at the Amex Stadium where learners have their achievements rewarded and celebrated. This taking of St. John's into the outside world was very much part of his style. He was an outward-looking Head, and knew full well, in the words of Mark Ryan, that a special school can quickly become isolated and inert unless steps are taken to engage with the outside world. Pupils and staff in other schools might regularly meet others through sports fixtures, debating competitions, say, or in myriad teenage parties and get-togethers that become part of the fabric of their lives. This is not the case at a special school or FE college. The very word autism refers to a condition where individuals are isolated from conventional social interaction. Learners have to be carefully managed to cope with relationships with each other and with the outside world. The whole process of acknowledgement, integral to a Graduation Ceremony, means a great deal to them and their parents.

'All heads of St. John's have put their thumb print on the school,' says Len Parkyn,[19] 'but Mark Hughes left a legacy of rare quality...If it had not been for Mark, we would be in a very different and difficult place now.'

Graduation at Amex (2017). The Graduation Ceremony is an acknowledgement and celebration of learners' achievements over their time at St. John's. (St. John's College)

19   Interview, 7 April 2018.

Chapter 7

Every child matters

IN THE SUMMER of 2016, Mark Hughes decided to move on, having done all that he felt he could at St. John's. There then followed a six-month interregnum, during which Karen Grist was the Acting Principal. In February 2017, Simon Charleton, already an experienced head, arrived to take up his post. In his first address to his staff he resurrected the title of a government green paper of 2003, 'Every Child Matters', to remind his staff of an essential truth about education, nowhere more relevant than in a special school.

Whereas Mark Hughes had an inspection after two years, Simon Charleton had a challenging Ofsted Report already waiting for him on his desk, the inspection having taken place at the end of January. The overall judgement was 'Requires Improvement', although both Personal Development and Outcomes for Learners were rated 'Good'. This latter judgement should have been no surprise, given the continual emphasis on the individual, and Mark Hughes' unflinching preoccupation with work experience. However, the stark fact was that the main area where the College was found wanting was in the most fundamental area of Teaching and Learning. Nevertheless, Richard Stewart, the Chairman, and Len Parkyn were disappointed that the inspectors were reluctant to acknowledge the considerable advances that had been made in establishing and following an appropriate curriculum. This outcome presented Simon Charleton with challenges that were to define the early months of his headship. Clearly the way in which lessons were planned, delivered and assessed would need a greater focus. St. John's went back to the basics: understanding how young people learn and then providing them with engaging and challenging lessons.

So much emphasis in educational debate these days is placed on the achievements of the top 40% of the pupil population, those who are going to achieve 'good' grades in at least five subjects at GCSE, including English and Maths, and then go on to take A levels and proceed to a university. Much less social and political debate is centred on those at the other end of the educational scale, those whose innate conditions prevent them performing at the same level as the majority of their peers, but whose achievements are in no less need of endorsement and celebration.

Any time spent in St. John's gives insight into what can be done through sheer dedication and hard work. As there is so much focus on identifying individuals'

The staff photographed in April 2018. (Ian Muir Photographer)

needs and on devising specific learning programmes, the teaching skills required are very different from the craft of the classroom practised by teachers in mainstream schools. The staffing ratio is also different at St. John's. Four hundred teaching, care and therapy staff look after 120 learners on the two sites. That is a remarkable ratio of three staff to each learner. In a mainstream school 12 learners to each member of staff would be a favourable ratio. This has an impact on the way staff see the School, and know their learners.

Commitment amongst all sectors of staff is palpable. Dennis Boxall speaks of getting the thumbs-up sign in Sainbury's one Sunday afternoon from a non-verbal learner whom he hadn't seen for a while. It made his day. Liz Coles came to St. John's in 2000 as a Receptionist. She was good at her work, enjoyed it and went on to take extra responsibilities as a PA to the Head of the College and to be in charge of Admissions at both School and College from 2008. What has made her stay? 'I like the way St. John's faces changes all the time, like new ideas coming through a revolving door, and the way change is embraced…It is such a creative place.' This openness to change and the continually creative outlook is clearly what sustains St. John's and ensures that every one of its learners is seen as special. Every child really does matter.

Part III

Building Futures

Simon Charleton, the current CEO of St. John's, reflects on what the School and College can offer in the next ten years:

When Jane Borradaile wrote in 1875 'I put forward no fresh plea as to the necessity of such institutions', the point that she then made, albeit using words that our 21st century dispositions might today find awkward, remains compelling. When our fund-raiser goes out and asks for support for the charity's work she is not making a fresh plea; she is asking good people to invest in the future of our young people, for without St. John's and other similar schools and colleges the lives of thousands of young people would be worse off and so much potential would be wasted.

Schools and colleges like St. John's should not need their case to be made. The young people and their families tell us every week how important we are in their lives and how, alongside our partners in the maintained sector, we are a key part of the 'local offer'.[20] The world is now more connected than in Jane Borradaile's day and young people come to St. John's from outside the South-East; from London, the North, Wales and indeed even from the Far East, so 'regional/national offer' might be a better term. In this last chapter of our history, like Jane Borradaile, I am not making a 'fresh plea' to justify St. John's, but I will try and link our past history with our future path.

The preceding chapters show how St. John's has evolved over time to meet the changing needs of young people. The next ten years will see St. John's change once more as needs change and social attitudes to disability change. In 2018 we published a short document for our commissioners called 'Service Developments' and under that rather prosaic title lay an ambitious ten-year plan to change the charity radically. Much of the history up to this point is about the buildings and, in Brighton, St. John's is an imposing Victorian building looming gently and kindly over part of East Brighton. However, the 2020s will be about the less tangible aspects of placements for our young people; the relationships that we help them build; and their learning in the community. It will be about developing relationships with other schools such as our good neighbours at Hamilton Lodge School for the Deaf, with whom we work closely, and Brighton College, with whom we share many personal links through Governors and Trustees. The glorious and rather quirky building in Kemp Town about which so many fascinating stories have been woven will always be the heart of

Simon Charleton, CEO, 2017–the present day. (Ian Muir Photographer)

20   Specialist education available in Brighton and Hove.

Picture of learners
on work experience
at the Bevy pub and
the Peace Café at
the Buddhist Centre
in Hove. (St. John's
College)

St. John's but the future of the charity will be more virtual and networked. Already our Involve learners[21] operate as a virtual college, developing their skills almost completely in the community and rarely actually in the building. Our focus on independence and employability means that much of our learning takes place in settings right across our wonderful and inclusive city rather than in the actual building itself. As a result, when inspectors come in now we often have to Facetime them or Skype them to our learners.

Growing provision for the youngest children so that they can be well supported in their primary phase and re-integrated back into a mainstream school for their secondary years is one of our projects for the coming years. Some of our adults have benefited enormously from year-round support and so we are opening, at our Seaford school, a similar homely and all-year placement. In the jargon it is known as a children's home but we see it as the children's home.

Increasingly, our young people are coming to us with a wider range of physical and mental health needs alongside their autism. The technical, and rather ugly, term for this is 'co-morbid'; we prefer the term 'complex'. Therefore, during 2017 and 2018 we invested heavily in increasing our skills in dealing with mental health as we want to take seriously the reclassification of the old Behavioural, Emotional and Social

Music-making in Resonance. (St. John's College)

21 Learners aged 16–22 who are unable, for a variety of reasons, to access learning in college. A team of 12 staff are involved in helping them to access the curriculum in the community.

Difficulties designation to the Social, Emotional and Mental Health designation. Our aim is to work with commissioners to prevent young people going into more acute mental health settings and also to provide a school for them to step down to when they leave these acute settings.

We also have our ambitious Building Futures project, which aims to raise £5 million, which will be used to fund the building of new classrooms and bedrooms for some of our most complex learners. It would be a touch hubristic to compare oneself to Jane Borradaile but I hope we too can leave a legacy of 'state of the art' education and care for our most complex young people. Some of these new projects will happen at our Seaford site, which also has a fascinating history and may, perhaps,

The language of disability

Few uses of language, except possibly for racism, have aroused such sensitivities as the words associated with disability. By the 1970s, even the word 'handicapped' had been replaced with the term 'disabled'. The former implies that life is a horse race in which some competitors are going to do less well because of a particular burden or flaw they have been handed. 'Disabled', or sometimes 'less abled' feels less judgemental; it is more of a statement of fact. In many ways descriptive language has become less about competition and judgement, and more about neutral description.

Even the original name of Jane Borradaile's institution contains a word that is unacceptable now: today, no one in any formal context would describe those suffering from a physical deformity as 'cripples'. Like many words used in the nineteenth century to describe a physical condition, these terms have often been devalued and used in a pejorative sense by children being cruel to one other. 'Moron', 'imbecile' and 'idiot' – all terms used to an intended jocular effect in the classroom or playground until comparatively recently – were once deemed valid descriptors in educational or psychiatric parlance. (They denoted the lowest IQ bands, namely 51–70, 26–50 and 0–25.)

'Spastic' was similarly hijacked to refer to physical weakness – or a general worthlessness. The Spastics Society continued blithely to refer thus to those suffering from cerebral palsy from its establishment in 1952 until 1994, when the anodyne term 'Scope' was substituted as one more in line with marketing and PR strategies.

So when did changes in attitudes to such language come about? The Handicapped Children Act of 1970 changed the provision of services from Health/Care to Education, which led to legislation pertaining to qualified staff and also appropriate language. However, it was the Warnock Report of 1978 that first addressed the whole question of educating 'children with learning difficulties' as opposed to those deemed to be 'educationally sub-normal' (the phrase used to describe St. John's School when it reopened in 1957). Requirements were subsequently placed on Local Education Authorities to make more provision for such children. Warnock was the 'Bible of what should be', in the words of one Trustee,[1] and remains influential today.

Over the next 25 years legislation was passed that addressed both recognition and inclusion, by way of the Disabled Persons Act of 1986, the International Salamanca Statement of 1994, about inclusion, and the Special Educational Needs and Disabled Act of 2001, which essentially spelt out the duties of all institutions in accommodating the disabled, and making it illegal to fail in those duties. The last quarter of the 20th century, then, saw vast changes in attitude, in terms of rights, signifying a shift towards a more sympathetic and sensitive use of language.

---

1 Len Parkyn, interview 7 May 2018.

one day become a Volume II to this current book. The parallels in terms of what was until 1997 the Pilgrims School, set up to provide support for young people with breathing difficulties, changing to meet the needs of young people with communication needs, are strikingly similar to the story of our Brighton site. In the world of education things change and, sometimes, this is a good thing. The change in attitude to disability is a good example of this.

Even during my working life terminology has changed. In one of my first schools we had a teacher in charge of 'remedial' children and then another school had an 'adjustment unit'. 'Naughty' children were sometimes hit by large adults with bamboo canes, inflicting significant harm; this was called 'corporal punishment' – nowadays it would be a criminal offence! 'Inclusion' became the buzz word for a bit in the 1990s and this worked well in some schools where children with complex needs were well catered for. However, inclusion could also mean exclusion, as large, busy, target-focussed schools couldn't adapt their setting to the needs of some learners with specific needs. Although the teachers were often caring and professional, the mindset was all about young people being a problem (or sometimes as damaging outliers on performance league tables) and needing to adjust rather than being seen as talented young people who need to discover ways to release these talents. At St. John's we relentlessly focus on what our young people can do and promote that rather than focussing on what they can't do.

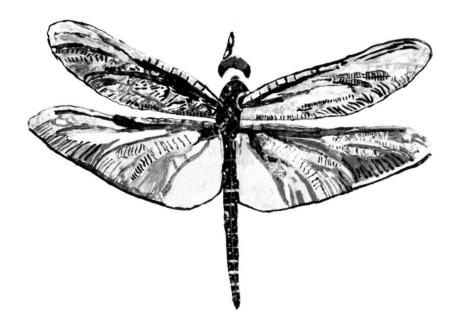

Kingfisher and dragonfly from Inklusion studio. (St. John's College)

91

Many of our young people and young adults are on the autism spectrum and thus see the world differently from their neuro-typical peers. Autism, along with other forms of communication difficulty, comes in many forms. There are education professionals up and down the country deciding which set of initials to put alongside the young person on their Education, Health and Care Plan in order to correctly to classify their needs. Whilst we give these labels appropriate consideration at St. John's – the needs of a person with Pathological Demand Avoidance are clearly distinct from those with Down's Syndrome – we simply focus on the behaviours and the needs of the young person rather than obsessing about the label that they have been given (Flo Longhorn described this as ABC XYZ Syndrome). St. John's always focuses on the positive. The great artwork from our Inklusion social enterprise is one of many examples of how our learners can produce wonderful work when given the opportunity.

A word on 'behaviour' might be helpful at this point. Traditionally, 'behaviour' has had a slightly negative connotation, hence schools for children with behavioural problems or more technically 'conduct disorders'. St. John's takes a different view, as we believe that behaviour is a neutral term which describes what we all do as a response to a stimulus or antecedent event. So recently when an inspector asked me: 'Please can I see your sanctions and punishments policy?' I was able to say, 'We don't have any sanctions or punishments' and move on to more interesting and positive discussions. This approach sometimes causes people to get the wrong end of the stick, if you will forgive the metaphor.

Some readers might remember the 'progressive' schools of the 60s and 70s such as Summerhill where, so the popular press told us, there were no rules and sanctions and pupils could do what they wanted. The St. John's approach is very different: we spend a lot of time teaching our learners about social rules and social norms and expectations; we have lots of routines and our settings are very calm and very well-ordered. The difference is that if a learner does something 'wrong', all our focus from then on is on understanding why they did it and how to help them manage their behaviours more effectively in the future. In one sense our approach is tougher than the punishment-based approach where there is little space for reflection and the sanction often stands in place of helping the learner understand social rules. Sanctions are quick fixes that rarely fix.

I was lucky in 2011 to visit the USA with an organisation called Project Search and spend time at the Cincinnati Children's Hospital meeting with a range of young adults with life stories very similar to those of our learners at St. John's. These young adults were all on Supported Internships in the hospital and some had progressed into full-time employment in the hospital. I met one young

Learner and pony getting to know each other in the Involve programme. (St. John's College)

lady, 'Ruth' we will call her, with Down's Syndrome, part of whose job was to ensure that surgeons had the correct number of scalpels and other tools of their trade in their packs in theatre. There were nearly 100 tools in the pack. Even I, coming from a background of working with young people with learning difficulties, raised a small section of eyebrow at being told this information! I assume it is quite important during heart surgery to have all the tools you need ready at hand. I was, however, reassured by hospital staff that Ruth's accuracy levels were consistently higher by 1–2% than those of her mainstream colleagues because of her ability to focus on a task where speed of completion was not vocationally relevant but accuracy was. Ruth had needed a lot of support during her late teens and early 20s to get this job and now she was a fully functioning member of society who at the end of her shift went to her own home – a supported living environment that enabled her to live as independently as possible – on the bus.

Christmas carol concert at St George's Church, 2017. (St. John's College)

The ground-breaking legislation of the Children and Families Act 2014 enshrined the provision for support for our learners up to the age of 25, but it is often after the age of 19 that people begin to question the need for education to continue. In Ruth's case it was the social investment by the State of Ohio at this time that enabled her to flourish. St. John's is passionate about all learners continuing to develop their knowledge and skills during these years, and every day at the College shows how important this is.

St. John's links all its work to five clear placement outcomes and the last of these is employability. We believe that all our young people should go on and gain meaningful employment or be enabled to employ their time meaningfully. Not all will gain full-time jobs like Ruth in Cincinnati, but the world of work is changing and there will be an employability niche in the gig economy or world of micro-enterprises for most of our leavers if we all try hard enough and never stop aiming for the stars.

Nobody questions the right of neuro-typical young people to go on and develop their minds at university – often miles away from their homes. Our parents and young people have similar expectations – and why not? Peter Imray, one of the sharpest and most thought-provoking writers in this area of work, once wrote an article called 'Saying No to No!' He was writing about a no sanctions policy and nicely summarises the St. John's approach to behaviour; the catch line applies to how we see the future for our learners after St. John's – there should be no barriers, only opportunities; no limits, only possibilities; no standing still, only going forward.

Appendix

St. John's Chairmen of the Trustees

1890   Col HC Grove Morris
1912   C Villiers Johnson
1947   H Christopher Mileham
1957   Tom Berry
1970   Olwyn Davies
1993   Leon Morton
1997–   Richard Stewart

St. John's Chairmen of the Governors

–2008   Jean Marshall
2008–   Len Parkyn

St. John's Heads

1928   Hilda Lindo (Headmistress)
1950   Margaret Walker (Headmistress)
1957   Chetwyn Butler (Headmaster)
1967   Dennis Forster (Headmaster)
1994   Mike Hudson (Principal)
2000   Don Kent (Chief Executive)
2010   Mark Hughes (CEO and Principal) (till 2016)
2017–   Simon Charleton (CEO and Principal)

Index